The Musakanya Papers

THE MUSAKANYA PAPERS

THE AUTOBIOGRAPHICAL WRITINGS OF VALENTINE MUSAKANYA

EDITED BY
MILES LARMER

Lembani Trust
LUSAKA

http://sites.google.com/site/lembanitrust/

First published 2010 by the Lembani Trust
Lusaka, Zambia

Editorial matter and introduction Copyright © Miles Larmer 2010
Text Copyright © Kapumpe-Valentine Musakanya 2010

ISBN 978-9982-9972-3-2

Typeset in Gentium

First, this book is dedicated to the emergence of a new Zambian spirit that is dedicated to accurate historical presentation and writing and to all those that will be encouraged by this book to write — for today and for the future.

Second, but not least, this book is dedicated to Flavia Musonda Musakanya; this completes you now. You waited painfully for so many years, without any reward, for a platform of reason and accuracy in which your husband's writings could be presented on unconditional terms.

Table of Contents

Foreword

The pages that follow reveal a process of transformation for one of Zambia's most curious intellects. Valentine Shula Musakanya was born in rural Zambia, but became identified with urban development. He started school at the very late age of thirteen, but in later life was seen as a young achiever. Certainly he found himself in unique circumstances when at the age of twenty-six he was not only happily married, with a son, but also occupied the top position in the Northern Rhodesia African Civil Service.

Musakanya's meteoric rise was made possible by supportive parents and positive role models like Harry Mwaanga Nkumbula. It is interesting that Musakanya's relationship with Nkumbula started on a rather sour note. Shortly after enrolling at Wusakile African School, Musakanya started playing truant and succeeded in avoiding classes for two months. Inevitably the game came to an end when the Attendance Officer reported that the new student had never attended classes. Musakanya senior then decided to personally take his son to school the following morning.

Had Valentine known what awaited him at the school, he might have been less nonchalant. On arrival at the headmaster's office, Musakanya senior demanded that his son be punished in his presence. Harry Mwaanga Nkumbula obliged, with rather more enthusiasm than young Valentine would have wished. According to Musakanya, the caning that followed was 'merciless'.

But Nkumbula was not a merciless person. After administering the punishment, he asked kindly, why Valentine had played truant. Musakanya's response was that he had felt insulted by being place in Sub A (the first grade of education) when he already knew how to read Bemba. Nkumbula was amused and decided to test the boy's reading himself. Musakanya fluently read the Bemba texts given him and earned an instant promotion to Sub B, and three months later, to Standard 1.

This was not the last time that Musakanya's academic career was fast tracked. This episode however helps explain how someone who started school at such a late age ended up achieving so much in a relatively short space of time. It also explains Musakanya's loyalty to Harry Mwaanga Nkumbula.

Many years later when the governing United National Independence

Party decided to withdraw recognition of the office of Leader of the Opposition, Musakanya, as Secretary to Cabinet, resisted moves to hastily evict Harry Nkumbula from the residence he occupied as Leader of the Opposition. Although Musakanya served as top civil servant in the UNIP government, he also maintained an excellent relationship with Harry Nkumbula. I know from personal experience that when Harry Nkumbula died, Valentine Musakanya was greatly saddened that he could not attend the funeral, on account of his incarceration by Zambia's first president.

That incarceration provides the sad backdrop to this book. Musakanya considered his detention by the one party state authority inevitable. Certainly his independence of mind and intellectual honesty would have made his relationship with Zambia's autocratic and duplicitous regime very difficult.

Valentine Shula Musakanya was nothing if not intellectually honest. A few years after Zambia's Independence, he was angered when members of the UNIP youth brigade went around cities threatening and even assaulting women wearing mini skirts. The campaign was launched in defence of traditional Zambian culture which, according to UNIP, did not permit short dresses. Musakanya could not help but observe that as a child in traditional rural Zambia his grandmother's clothing was so scant that she was practically nude.

Musakanya was not necessarily in favour of mini skirts. He was however concerned about distorting Zambian history for the sole purpose of justifying Government or Party policy. He was further concerned about Government involvement in what he saw as trivial matters to be dealt with by individuals and families. Musakanya saw Government's willingness to romanticise Zambian culture and history and willingness to get involved in trivial matters of personal choice as the beginning of the abdication of responsibility, especially at a time when it was plausible to blame all ills on the recently departed colonial administration. This in turn led to the belief that every problem created in the post-colonial era was temporary and easily solvable.

Musakanya's foresight is evident throughout this book and certainly when he comments on the then rare but noticeable practice of building poorly designed houses in areas not zoned for residential purposes. Whereas the official position was that these structures would not last long and the occupants would eventually find proper accommodation elsewhere, Musakanya recognised the structures as the beginnings of towns and suburbs. His suggestion was that while these settlements were still small and manageable, Government should take services to them as the only effective way of preventing the mushrooming of slums. He summarised his position with the phrase;

'Towns are not made, they become'.

Unfortunately this idea was dismissed. Other ideas were better received, however. Valentine was more successful in his promotion of science and technology. He established the Zambia Air Services Training Institute which was responsible for producing a large number of well trained Zambian pilots, shortly after Independence. He also created a network of colleges of technology across the country. Perhaps he is best remembered for the Nshimatic, designed to cook Nshima on a large scale, and popular with institutions like hospitals.

It is regrettable that not a single avenue, street, road, building, airport, or institution has been named after Valentine Shula Musakanya. We must hope that this timely tribute to one of Zambia's most innovative sons will be followed by official recognition of Mr. Musakanya's contribution to Zambia.

NC Puta-Chekwe
July 2008

Acknowledgements

Valentine Shula Musakanya left his writings with me prior to his death. It was always going to be a challenge to find collaborators who would enable the publication of his works. He was stooped in history and there were few reference points and avenues for these works in Zambia. I met Miles Larmer whilst he was engaged in his academic work on sub-saharan Africa. It was a natural development and I must confess that due to the depth of his research and knowledge on Zambia and VSM, it was occasionally a student-teacher relationship. Dr Larmer has pursued this publication to a point where most people would have given up, after many years of frustrating trips to Zambia on limited budgets and running into closed doors. He was nevertheless able to identify something that motivated him. Miles introduced me to the wonderfully like-minded people, the publishers of Lembani Trust, without whom this book could not have been possible: Marja Hinfelaar, Giacomo Macola and Lawrence Dritsas for the type-setting, and others who made such efforts for the passion of the history and for Zambia. I marvel at how such a combination of chance, charity and perfection in a working relationship came to being. I would also like to thank my brother Shula for the effort in obtaining the photos. I thank you all for making this book possible and so does my late father.

.

EDITOR'S INTRODUCTION

Valentine Shula Musakanya (1932-1994) was one of the leading Zambian political and intellectual figures of his generation. He played a crucial role in shaping the country's national institutions during the First Republic (1964-1972), serving as Secretary to the Cabinet and Secretary General to the Government; Minister of State for Technical and Vocational Education; and as Governor of the Bank of Zambia during this period. He was regarded as one of the country's most able and intelligent leaders and was widely thought of as a potential future President of Zambia.

Today, however, Musakanya is generally remembered neither in connection with his achievements in government and administration, nor for his subsequent business successes in the 1970s, when he worked in a senior position with the multinational computing corporation IBM. Rather, his legacy is irretrievably marked by his involvement in the attempted coup which was pre-empted, in October 1980, by the arrest of those alleged to be involved, Musakanya included. After a lengthy and controversial legal process, in 1983 Valentine Musakanya was convicted, along with seven others, of treason and sentenced to death. However, in 1985, Musakanya was acquitted following his appeal to the Supreme Court, on the basis that the sole evidence against him was a confession which, it was acknowledged, had been extracted through the use of torture. After his release, he lived on in Lusaka for a further decade before his death in 1995.

For myself, as an academic researcher seeking to explain the actions and motivations of leading political figures in post-colonial Zambia, Musakanya has appeared to be something of a mystery. How could this highly intelligent, sophisticated and cosmopolitan figure, so committed to democratic governance, modern political practice and the rule of law, have become engaged in an attempt to overthrow by force of arms a sovereign government, albeit one whose authority rested on the repressive institutions of a one-party state? In interviewing Musakanya's friends and former colleagues, it became clear that they also found it difficult to imagine how the eloquent and urbane Musakanya, at ease with international statesmen and business figures, became engaged with a secretive and unavoidably violent plot. One answer to this riddle was simply that Musakanya was indeed innocent of involvement, as he had been found by the courts. This publication, whilst not providing a definitive account of the coup plot, suggests in contrast that Musakanya played an important role in the early stages of the conspiracy, although this had significantly diminished in importance by the time the physical organisation of the plot neared completion in the second half of 1980.

Readers will wish to know whether the private papers of Valentine Musakanya, available in this volume for the first time, provide an answer to the mystery of his involvement in the coup attempt. The answer is perhaps both yes and no. Although a great deal of light is shed on the organisation of the coup attempt (utilising not only Musakanya's own writings, but also the editor's own archival research and interviews with other protagonists), Musakanya himself does not provide a blow-by-blow explanation of the extent of his own involvement in the plot. This is hardly surprising—much of this material was written at a time when Musakanya was in prison, accused and later convicted of treason and facing possible execution. Even those documents written after Musakanya's release were prepared in the last years of the United National Independence Party's 'one-party participatory democracy'; the author was therefore not in a position to reveal all aspects of his involvement in an attempt to overthrow that political system. It must be concluded, therefore, that some secrets in this regard went to the grave with Valentine Musakanya himself, and are unlikely ever to be revealed. Musakanya never wrote about his personal experience of torture, explaining to his family that it was too traumatic to describe and believing that writing down his experiences would not be cathartic. He did however believe that, in some way, the spirit of his ancestors would find a way of delivering retribution and justice to his torturers. Although those who ordered and carried out his torture (and those of other Zambians during the one-party state era) have not been tried and convicted in a Zambian courtroom, it is hoped that this publication will go some way to highlighting his suffering and thereby deliver a form of justice to Musakanya, his immediate family and his ancestors.

In a different way, however, these writings provide a clear and compelling explanation of how Musakanya came to be involved in the 1980 coup attempt. This is because they chart his early and profound unhappiness with the nature of post-colonial politics in Zambia; his attempts to guard against the growth of patronage, corruption, populism and authoritarianism; his anger at the utilisation of national resources for personal gain; and his sense of betrayal at the opportunities squandered for democratic advancement, national development and prosperity. Musakanya's critique, expressed here not only in retrospective memoirs, but also in policy documents and contemporaneous correspondence with his colleagues in government and administration in the 1960s and early 1970s, is one of the most eloquent analyses of what went wrong with the project of national independence, not only in Zambia, but also in much of sub-Saharan Africa. As such, it certainly helps explain that Musakanya's path towards extra-legal resistance to the UNIP one-party state had its foundation in a widely shared sense of discontent with the repressive and corrupt nature of that political system, which had its origins in the authoritarian forms of governance adopted by UNIP even during the First Republic. Indeed, this editor would argue that the importance of Musakanya's writings goes far beyond the events of 1980; rather, they can best be interpreted as an instructive history of the challenges and failures of governance throughout the formerly colonial world.

Preparing these papers for publication was no easy task. Musakanya's writings encompass dozens of documents and thousands of pages (his unedited autobiography alone extends to 220,000 words), covering a series of overlapping themes and arguments. After much preparatory work, it has been decided to present this work in two main sections.

Musakanya's autobiography, presented here in edited form, provides for the most part a narrative account of his life and times, from his birth in a Northern Province village in 1932 (Chapter 1), through his brilliant but unorthodox educational career (Chapters 2 and 3), his appointment as Northern Rhodesia's first African District Officer (Chapter 5), and his position at the acme of the post-Independence administration in 1964 (Chapter 7). Subsequent chapters examine his relations with leading political figures and his attempts to fulfil his successive roles in government, administration and business (Chapters 8-11). This exposition is characteristically well written, but uneven, with extensive detail on his early life and career, but with later passages digressing into examinations of particular issues and problems (for example, in Chapter 12).

It has therefore been decided to supplement the edited manuscript with additional background material. Written by the editor, these interventions are presented in a regular font and are intended to frame and further explain Musakanya's analysis of particular issues. Musakanya's own writings, which make up the vast majority of the text, are written in the first person and presented in italics with indented paragraphs or, when quoted by the editor in his notes, in italics and inverted commas.

Musakanya himself provides a compelling account of his arrest and detention at the hands of state forces (Chapter 14), but not, as noted, a full explanation of his involvement in the coup attempt, nor of the events of the coup plot itself. This is addressed in Chapter 13, in which the editor draws on his own research into the events of 1980. Whilst this is an unconventional form of autobiographical writing, it is an approach which the publishers believe best serves the material available and which preserves the essence of Musakanya's own aims in preparing this manuscript. In contrast to some recently published memoirs of Zambian political leaders, Musakanya's aim was not an exercise in self-praise nor the scoring of points against his enemies, but rather a rigorous and self-critical examination of the problems of post-colonial government which would enable the learning of lessons and the avoidance of similar mistakes.

The second major part of this publication consists of significant policy statements, documents, or correspondence, in which Musakanya examines a range of events and issues of central importance to post-colonial Zambian history. Some of these shed new light on well-known events, such as the political tensions at UNIP's 1967 Conference (Appendix 6) and the economic reforms of the First Republic (Appendices 2, 10 and 11). Other documents explore less-examined areas of central concern to Musakanya, in particular the distortion of the neutrality of the civil service and state finances for party political ends in the decade after independence (Appendices 1, 4, 5 and 9). A further set of papers explore the personality and ideas of President Kenneth Kaunda, and those who influenced the development of 'Zambian Humanism', particularly Colin Morris (Appendices 7 and 8). Musakanya, himself an avid student of ideas and philosophy, was highly critical of the intellectual vacuity of 'Humanism' and its proponents, and regarded the development of such national philosophies as a dangerous step towards creating cults of personality around African Presidents which undermined free thinking and democracy (Appendix 12 provides particular insight in this regard). Musakanya's critique of the post-colonial state is in acute contrast to the nationalist literature celebrating the achievements of Zambia's First Republic. It is a particularly powerful analysis because it is provided by someone at the heart of the decision-making processes. Musakanya's identification of the systematic utilisation of government resources for political ends; the 'purchasing' of senior politicians by western businessmen; the ways in which development planning bypassed democratic politics; and the manipulation of the masses in the name of African nationalism, is a compelling one of considerable historical value.

Taken together, the papers of Valentine Musakanya provide an unprecedented, if highly personalised, insight into the achievements and failures of politics and governance in independent Zambia. They will also help readers understand the complex and ambiguous personality of Valentine Musakanya himself, and thereby give some insight into the apparent paradox of his limited involvement in the events of 1980. Musakanya's hopes and aspirations for his newly independent country came under early and sustained pressure, frustrated by alternative visions of what nationalist governance would involve. What Musakanya saw as the development of an efficient and politically neutral civil service was, for many new politicians, the continuation of 'colonial' rule. What was for Musakanya the corrupt patrimonial distortion of government expenditure was, for many UNIP activists, the just reward for their struggle for independence. Musakanya's admitted naivety in regard to post-colonial power, and his distaste for mass politics, was coupled with his mistaken belief that he could use the power of his intellect, to convince his political masters through the sheer bravura of his exposition. The limited purchase of an ability he had been taught to value above all else, a talent which had taken him, the son of a mineworker, to one of the highest offices in the land, contributed to his frustration and outspokenness.

Musakanya's obstinate refusal to kowtow to UNIP's fragile supremacy, his achievement of prestigious international employment and the independence this gave him from Presidential patronage, made him an unusual and particularly dangerous opponent of the 'party and its government'. From the late 1960s onwards, UNIP identified Musakanya and his friends and colleagues, Zambia's independent-minded lawyers, businessmen and intellectuals, as unpatriotic dissidents who needed to be taught that there was no room in post-colonial Zambia for their overt criticism. Musakanya's association with this group, and his preparedness to engage in what he may have regarded as idle talk regarding the removal of the President, suggests an impatient and at times arrogant individual whose courage in confronting his enemies was matched by a disregard for practical political realities.

Musakanya was alienated from most Zambians by his education and westernisation, something he appears to have been ambivalent about throughout his life—he embraced learning, both secular and spiritual, but that learning hamstrung him in his personal relations with the community he sought to serve. If his attitude to the masses is at times conservative and patrician, his analysis of Zambia's post-colonial ruling class is more radical, resembling at times Frantz Fanon's acerbic critique of the ostentatious consumption of national wealth by post-colonial African elites. Valentine Musakanya believed that the Zambian people deserved an independent state which was every bit as good as those of Western Europe, that such a state was entirely achievable, and dedicated much of his physical and intellectual energy to the fulfilment of this goal. He rejected notions that Africa should pursue paths of development distinct to what he regarded as universal norms of human advancement, and the idea that external constraints on African development should serve as an excuse for unaccountable and inefficient administration or political corruption. His unwillingness or inability to engage with the messy realities of everyday politics prevented him from providing a practical challenge to UNIP's weaknesses; as a consequence, he became partially involved in a reckless project to remove Kaunda from power. This was the tragedy of a distinctive and extraordinary life, a story which provides real insight into the nature of the post-colonial African state and its intellectual discontents.

Miles Larmer

INTRODUCTION

The following is Valentine Musakanya's own introduction to his autobiographical writing, which he began whilst in detention:

Today, 19th July 1981, I find myself making these notes before a kerosene lamp (an apparatus I last used over thirty years ago) in Chipata prison, have been flown here this morning from Lusaka Prison for the second time in nine months. I have been detained on an allegation of 'plotting' to overthrow by force of arms, the Kaunda Government of Zambia. I cannot say that this has been the most painful period of my life so far, but it is certainly the most thought-provoking. I would think that if it had not happened my life would have been incomplete, even with death. [...] In the quiet [...] that prison has afforded me, I have tried to recast my mind on my past, and piece together some memories into what has led me to where I am sitting. Surveying before me the meandering Luangwa as it rushes into the Zambezi coiling amidst the hills, I sang the Te Deum as I look at this as yet unspoilt African beauty, because I have concluded that I have had an especially good life; it may even be unique for it has not only spanned my years but also a leap of certain cultures and environments.

Born in the lion-haunted village of Lubemba; saved from the rampant delinquency of the semi-urbanisation of the Copperbelt Mine Compounds; starting school at the age of thirteen, thirteen years later I not only had a University Degree (an almost unheard of thing among us at the time) but also a wife I loved, a baby boy, and a position at the top of the African Civil Service in Colonial Northern Rhodesia! Ten years later I [...] became head of the Zambian Civil Service soon after Independence. Another ten years later I had been initiated in (or is it tainted with?) politics by having been an MP (nominated) and a Minister; Governor of the Bank of Zambia; and an Executive in a high-technology multi-national corporation, of which I became the only black General Manager of its operations in Africa. Now in my fifth decade, I have successfully had a go at business on my own account, in the midst of which I was plucked on 24 October 1980 to add to my experience that of a prison graduate. Whether this was inevitable, for good or bad, the future will tell.

This synopsis compresses some thirty years, a life beginning from virtually iron-age surroundings, through to the explosion of the electronic age, not merely as a bystander but as a participator. It has meant crushing classes, cultures and technologies many centuries ahead of my individual beginnings. Such meteoric acceleration and exposure should leave its bruises, and peculiarise a character into a synthesis of the originating past and the living present. One example is that I cannot tell my past in its original medium — my mother tongue. [...] Thus there is the risk of expressing or experiencing the past and the present through a wrong medium. These stresses I have experienced in my relationships with my parents, local relatives and some local politicians on the one hand, and with my western contacts on the other [...] one suffers both extremes of being overestimated and underestimated.

In retrospect, this smooth sailing denied me a personal experience of competitiveness, or what may be called political manoeuvring to gain position or favours. I have unconsciously felt that I was above competition, that I would get there on merit. One caution recurred in my matriculation reports: "Be more competitive, to ensure a first class pass." [...] It is not that I disapprove of competitiveness and ambition, on the contrary I have approved and encouraged them in others. But it has not been at any time necessary in my own case, and I never thought that other people's competition and ambition could hurt me. [...]

I suppose that the above synopsis of success inevitably created some enemies, even of the system itself. Moreover, when one moves rapidly as I have done, one tends to regard that progress as natural and to ignore that moving force of the unsuccessful and the helplessly ambitious. Envy may turn a friend into a foe, an erstwhile pupil into a traitor. All these are life's hazards and to locate them, where I can, I will search [...] my trail. This is not an autobiography in the conventional sense, but a review of the passage of events as they have vitally affected my role in them. Essentially events mean people because they, more often than not, cause them, and always they are affected by them. In my life there have been many people, some who taught and helped me, others who set examples for me to emulate, and those, more important, who have loved me. So telling my story is in fact telling part of the stories of so many other people. [...] I need hardly point out that objectivity has a contentious place in an autobiography, therefore omissions are as acceptable as inclusions, but truth must be subject only to the relativity of memory. It must, however, be interesting to read and, as much as possible, to provide useful and historical perspective on the period in which that life was lived — call it a novel of the unimaginative. Perhaps this is what it should be, because an accurately analytically executed autobiography would ring false against a canon of human nature, that we humans are so complex that it is nigh on impossible to understand ourselves as well as we might understand others.

1

EARLY LIFE IN THE VILLAGE AND THE TOWN
1932–50

*I was born in 1932 at Nkunkulusha's village in Kalundu country of Bembaland [...]
Kalundu is that large piece of land to the west of Kasama. [...] The land is a
watershed between Lukulu and Lubasenshi on the one hand and the Bangweulu
on the other. It is a low plateau from which perennial cool and really beautiful
streams, protected by magnificent tree groves called Mishitu, flow into these two
rivers. Administratively, it is ruled by Chief Munkonge who by tradition should be
the son of a chief — either Mwamba or Chitimikulu himself.*[1]

*Due to this background of custom, I was born with a birth family name of Shula
but also others for guardian spirits — Lupando, Mulenga. So my first full names
are Shula Malindi Lupando Mulenga Musonda Kapumpe Nkunkulusha etc etc. I
am Musakanya by my step-father, as my blood father died before I was born and
my mother remarried when I was under three years old. [...] I had no idea about it
because in our society my relatives would avoid telling about it to a youngster.*[2]

*All I [...] have been told is that soon after marriage, my father, as was the
custom in the early 'thirties, went off with his friends to look for fortune in order
to return and look after his family. They went to Mpiwe (in Tanganyika) to work
on some diamond mines there. He was under 20, the youngest of the team, and had
not been gone for many months when word came that he had died. My mother was
pregnant, but notwithstanding that, my father's family concluded that somehow
she was responsible for his death [...] by the time I was born the feud had already
reached boiling point, such that my father's relatives did not want to know me [...]
fearing continued persecution and the certainty of my being bewitched, [my
mother], her twin brother, and her maternal grandmother became fugitives, and
left our family village to which they never returned. They went to Matunda on the*

---

[1] Valentine Musakanya, 'Biographical Manuscript', pp. 1-5. All further references to this manuscript will be
by page number only.
[2] p. 10.

banks of the Lubansenshi and near to the Bangweulu swamps.

As I grew up, I had a remarkable resemblance to my father, which [led] my father's family to make some reconciliation. It was too late, and the feud continued. [...] I had no reason to believe in this resemblance until a few years ago when, well over forty years old, I decided to make my own reconciliation by going to see my father's people at Nkunkulusha. I took my daughter with me and on the way told her that nobody would recognise me because no-one at that village had seen me since I was six years old. [...] When we arrived we advanced to the nearest house where a woman was standing outside; as we came closer, she stood rigid, clapped her mouth with her hands, and shook all over before screaming, calling my late father's name. [...] She was, as it happened, the late sister of my father.[3]

I have very faint memories of my childhood in the village and all that I remember was that both my mother and my [step-]father were not there; they were already on the Copperbelt. [...] However, certain aspects and events of village life stand out in my mind well enough, because I must have been ten years old when I was taken away. The life rotated around hunting and fishing; chitemene and reaping of millet; beer feasts and dancing; weddings and deaths, and the accompanying talk and accusations of witchcraft. I have reflected upon these with interest and I have found perfectly logical explanations, despite their being dubbed 'pagan' by early missionaries or 'primitive' practices by anthropologists.[4]

In his memoirs, Musakanya explains the fishing and hunting traditions of his community, illustrating the abundance of natural resources amongst which he grew up. He recounts his mother's tale of his near death following a crocodile attack during a fishing expedition, following which he was barred from attending such events. His uncle, the first born to his maternal grandmother, possessed the only gun in the area and would regularly hunt game for the family:

He was the most individualistic member of my family I have known. He never joined beer parties (he drank alone); he never sat at Nsaka (a village club); and he went hunting alone, occasionally with me carried on his shoulders when I could no longer walk. [...] I was his only nephew and he had only daughters. I was therefore his only successor and his absolute favourite. [...] I was absolutely spoilt by him [...] he always provided what I wanted to eat. [...] When he died he left me the gun, although he never saw me as a grown-up.[5]

Following his grandmother's death, Musakanya family moved back to Nkunkulusha, without his parents, to live with his other relatives:

[3] pp.13-15.
[4] pp. 17-18.
[5] p. 27.

As I remember it, it was over a hundred houses and divided into sections (ifitente) roughly along age groups. It even had a church where prayers were said every evening and children were taught catechism by one of my grandfathers, Mr Shimio Chipanta. From Mutanda, it was like going to an urban area, with lots of children and games.[6]

In this society, Musakanya's family was comparatively well off, able to eat meat on a regular basis; he noted the inequalities in consumption amongst families in the village.

From a very young age I was regarded as having a good memory, sometimes embarrassingly so; when my grandmother would say something that should not be repeated she would send me away because many months later I could repeat word for word what had been said. However this was in my favour, because many in the village would send me to deliver invitations for private dinners or beer parties. At a private dinner I would eat together with the elders.[7]

Musakanya depicts the role of the local 'nganga', as well as that of spirit mediums:

I distinctly remember one incident. I was coming from somewhere with my mother and uncle along a path, it must have been in the dry season because there was no tall grass. We saw a lion, not fifty yards from the path. It roared at us and threw chunks of earth with its back legs. My mother put me on her shoulders and went in front whilst my uncle followed behind (he had a spear). The lion followed at a 'respectable' distance. When we got to the village we found everybody worried and anxiously looking in the direction from where we had been expected. We were told that 'Lupando' (my guardian spirit, whose medium was one of my grandmothers) had warned that we were moving through a dangerous area where there was a man-eating lion and that 'he' (the spirit) had to accompany us home. Up to now I have not been able to find a satisfactory answer for this.[8]

Now and again a White Father came on tour, spent a night in the church and said Mass the following morning before pressing on elsewhere. The white father was the first white man I saw. [...] At Nkunkulusha by dint of family connections I automatically became a catechumen in my grandfather's church, which he was very anxious to fill. Few elders seemed concerned about going to church. Although most of the village turned up to listen to the priest when he came [...] whenever asked when they would be baptised, they would vaguely say that they were considering it. [...] They nevertheless encouraged their young to go to church and

[6] p. 28.
[7] p. 34.
[8] pp. 40-41.

be baptised.[9]

After I memorised grandfather's questions and answers for the catechism and prayers too well for his expectations, he decided that I should go to Mulabola Mission for final preparations for baptism as soon as possible [...] this was in 1942. [...] The 'course' was to last a month and we had to carry rations to last us through that period. [...] Mulobola Mission [...] looked a massive place to me because of the buildings: the Church, the Fathers' residence and the School with its dormitories. We found many people who had arrived from other villages and many more were still arriving [...] our classes were held in the church by a father, alternating with one school teacher. [...] After a week I was found to know the catechism by heart, and the Father began to take me from the lessons to go with him, visiting the mission garden he maintained and supervised. He would now and again take me to the mission residence and teach me to read from a Bemba primer. I quickly 'memorised' the primer and he gave me a new one as a present. [Because of this] [a]part from the first week I hardly attended the catechism classes. I only showed up in the last few days to practice for confession and communion.[10]

I returned to the village not only baptised [...] in that one month, I was acknowledged as literate [...] I became quite a sensation in the village being the only child who could read. [...] I also developed an obsession for books or any reading matter, but soon realised that I could only read those which had been 'read' to me. [...] There was only one answer—going to school and have more books read to me! But the nearest school was some twenty miles away at Kasakula village. [...] Because of the distance only the very oldest boys would go and would have to spend a week sleeping there and returning on Fridays.[11]

School attendance was not always popular in the village, depriving it of much needed labour.

One day, almost a year after my baptism, the Chief's Kapaso came to the village. His mission was to encourage, if not force, the boys to go to school at Kasakula. It will be noted that girls were not included, because it was traditionally out of the question to let a girl out of sight for the period required to attend that school [...] on his arrival, most eligible boys had disappeared from the village. [...] I was not hidden because my aunt and grandparents knew there was a possibility of me being accepted. The Kapaso [...] explained as well as he knew (he was himself illiterate) why the boys should be allowed to go to school and that if they did not do so the Chief might have to force them. Four or five boys who were present volunteered and, running off from my aunt's side, I went forward to the Kapaso,

[9] p. 44.
[10] pp. 45-47.
[11] pp. 47-48.

saying that I would also be going to school. There was laughter all around, and the Kapaso told me that I was too small to be able to make the journey. [...] When I insisted with tears, he consolingly agreed that I would be allowed to go, but he was convinced I would later be talked out of it, or would realise the difficulty after one trip. But I was determined to go and my aunt knew it.

When the day came, I was one of the six who went to school. My aunt cried bitterly to restrain me, as I cried bitterly to be let go. For my aunt [...] it was a double blow to love and responsibility: she had no child of her own, and I filled that place; in the absence of my mother, she might be accused of irresponsibility should harm come to me. But I went, carrying little food and without anything to cover myself at night [...] at Kasakula we found boys from other villages, and had to make small fires as soon as we arrived in the evening to cook our own food. We were not more than twenty who had come from other villages, who were like weekly boarders.[12]

Schooling [...] was mostly reading, writing (on the floor of the thatch-roofed classroom open on both sides), and some arithmetic. Very little time was spent in class in a day, because in addition to working in the teacher's garden and sweeping the school area, we had to have enough time for cooking and drawing water from the stream which was a good distance away. [...] The teacher, who alone taught sub-O, A, B, and Standard 1, was not too sure of himself and therefore did not like class work. He spent a good deal of time teaching catechism, in which he was so much at home that he did not care if it ate into the time set for the other subjects. [...] I looked forward to and enjoyed the lessons in my sub-O class. After a few weeks the teacher was highly impressed by my apparent reading ability, to which I quickly added fluent recital of arithmetic, so I was moved to sub A. The fact that I could not write did not seem to worry the teacher.[13]

It was, I think, after one or two terms that a man-eating lion nicknamed 'Namweleu' (so named because of its 'whirlwind' speed) started a career of terrorism in the area. He would catch and eat a person in one village and do the same in another village forty or fifty miles away a few hours later. As a result, we could not go to school. The whole of Kalundu was under siege. Cultivation and travel came to a standstill. [...] Many a time, a luckless traveller was chased by Namweleu into the village in broad daylight, only to find the village deserted as everybody was indoors. He would be caught and eaten in the village whilst the frightened villagers heard the screams and the cracking of bones; no one dared to go out to rescue the victim.

It was at this time that an uncle took me with him to the bush. [...] He 'lost' me

---

[12] pp. 48–50.
[13] p. 51.

and returned to the village. Having not returned to the village by 3pm, I was in the prevailing circumstances presumed dead and the villagers began barricading themselves indoors. There was no question of setting up a search party. Somehow I found my way to the village before dark, half dead from fear because I had seen a lion following me until very close to the village. My aunt had already begun mourning. The following day 'Lupando' came in the medium of my grandmother and reprimanded my uncle, who was accused of having deliberately abandoned me in the bush. She said I would have been eaten by Namweleu had she, Lupando, not guarded me to the village. This incident added to my insistence on going to school when I was considered too young — so my aunt concluded that I was not safe at the village and should therefore be sent to my father and mother on the Copperbelt. There I would go to school in safety and away from my late father's relations. In early 1944, my mother returned to the village expressly to take me with her to Nkana [Kitwe].[14]

I was so excited by the trip that I cannot recall any remorse about leaving friends and relatives in the village, who I would not see again for another twenty years. We had to trek from the village to the main Kasama–Luwingu road to find transport to the Copperbelt, which took a day of walking. The road was just being cut; its width and straightness made it a marvel for locals and it was named 'Lengelano', meaning 'the endless view'. It was the first major development project in Northern Province. With the severe shortage of mechanical equipment during the war, extensive manual labour was used, providing an employment boost along the way. Paradoxically, 'Lengelano' accounted for a large exodus of manpower from Northern Province during and after its construction (1943-1950), providing the wages needed for travelling to the mines. Job seekers no longer needed to laden themselves with ready rations for the trip, but instead travelled light with money to buy food along the route and catch a lift. After its completion traffic became regular and bus transport became available.[15]

As soon as we arrived, I was fascinated by the many big buildings, and by the vastness of the area, without many trees and grass nearby as was the natural appearance to me hitherto. Another new phenomenon was the large number of people I saw, none of whom my mother knew. My idea had been that the Copperbelt would just be a larger village [...] and that all the people would be known to my parents as was the case at the village. [...] I was quick to ask my mother the names of persons passing by or in a crowd, to which she irritably replied that she did not know many people in Kitwe. This really puzzled me, and this was compounded when I realised that we did have relatives in Kitwe, but they lived far

---

[14] pp. 51-2.
[15] p. 62.

away from our house, which was No. 144 in C7 section of Wusakile mine compound. Those who were our neighbours did not come from Nkunkulusha; in fact some spoke languages other than Bemba.[16]

Wusakile was a vast, treeless habitat of tens of thousands of people in 2,000 box-like corrugated roof huts standing in rows one after another. It was a new African mine compound or township built since the beginning of the war. The decision to build the new housing was expedited by the African strike of 1939 [sic, 1940]. *[...] Previously, the mines did not cater for African labour with families; miners had to leave their wives at the village. Were it not for the intervention of the Second World War, the situation would have possibly continued like this and the history of Zambia could have accordingly been different. The advent of the war increased demand for copper as a strategic metal, but at the same time reduced the flow of European labour to the mines. In the circumstances, the high turnover of African labour induced by the non-availability of family accommodation became an obstacle to the war effort. The* [1940] *disturbances further emphasised African labour instability. Thus, the mines began to encourage employees to have their families join them and started building 'appropriate' housing. Wusakile was built between 1940 and 1942 for married employees, leaving the old compound exclusively for bachelors.*[17]

As soon as was practical, I was taken to the Changa Changa. [the European mine official in charge of Wusakile] *My mother had to report that she was back from 'leave' (as regards freedom of movement and other controls, wives and children were treated like employees) and to register me for rations purposes. Naturally the place was strange to me, but I soon found many relatives around and from this point of view, the place began to take on a home look. At night I was absolutely fascinated by the electric lights which allowed us to play late in the evening. In the first few days I became a centre of attention for the other children who played by the lamp post. They were fascinated by the Bemba I spoke, which they thought was especially good; they also laughed at my pronunciation of 'shi' as 'ci'. I kept them there for long evenings telling stories, of which I appeared to have an enormous stock.*[18]

There was at that time compulsory education on the Copperbelt. Accordingly, I had to be presented to the school as soon as possible. I was taken to Wusakile African School, where Mr Thawe was taking over from Mr Harry Nkumbula as Headmaster. I went on the first day and thereafter faithfully moved with the early morning stream of school-going children, only to turn away with friends into the

---

[16] pp. 63-64
[17] pp. 66-68
[18] pp. 73-74.

nearby bush to trap birds. We would be back by the end of the day's school session to join the others going home. I played truant in this way for a couple months, until the Attendance Officer reported that I had never attended school. My father, who was on a night shift, promised to take me to school the following morning. [...] When we reached the school, I was led directly to the Headmaster's office, where he demanded that I be punished in his presence forthwith. I was mercilessly caned by Mr Nkumbula. He was somewhat soft afterwards and tried to console me, asking me why I did not like going to school. In defiance, I had the courage to tell him that it was because they put me in Sub A when I already knew how to read. He laughed and brought out some Bemba text which he gave me to test my reading. With much annoyance and injured pride I read (recited!) every chapter given to me from Sub A to Standard I books. They were very impressed with my reading and my diction. The Headmaster said that they should first try me in Sub B. I was quite happy with this decision.[19]

After three months in Sub B it was decided to move me to Standard I. This frightened me because I did not really know how to write and there would be an examination in four months time. Accordingly I began staying at home when not at school, just to practice writing. I failed Standard I and had to repeat in the 1945/46 school year. I soon found the trick to writing and took the lead in the class. In 1946 I went to Standard II and in 1947 to Standard III, still top of the class. After four months, I was promoted to Standard IV. There was a row about this, but quite a few of my teachers thought I was ready for the Standard IV examination. I passed Standard IV in May 1948 with nearly 100% marks.

This turning of a new leaf may sound rather dramatic but given the circumstances I do not think it was. Firstly I was given a tremendous morale boost by the promotions, and wished to meet the challenge. Secondly, that period at Wusakile and perhaps the other Copperbelt towns saw a new spirit of pride in and desire for education. This was probably due to the arrival at the school of a new team of newly trained teachers, amongst who were Matthew Mwendapole and Simon Kapwepwe. At first they were not accepted by the Copperbelt community, who regarded them as villagers (BaKamushi), [but] they provided a group to emulate for the young who wanted education. Mr Weston Chipaka found me in Standard II and took an instant liking to me. He asked my parents if I could stay with him and help cook for him, in return for which he would teach me more after school. My parents agreed and I lived with him until 1948. He was an enormously kind man from Petauke [...] he took over all parental responsibilities. [...] At £3.10 per month he earned twice as much as my father and he used to buy me lots of clothes.

---

[19] pp. 75-77.

This, plus what I earned as the only newspaper boy in town, made me very well off in the context of the time. Since I lived in the school compound, all the teachers came to know and like me. The majority of them were bachelors, and they took advantage of my knowledge of the compound to send me to deliver mail to their girlfriends and prospective wives. I also became close to Mr Emilio Mulalani, primarily because he was the choir master at the nearby Catholic parish church and also a class teacher in Standard II. Mulalani was easily the brightest of the teachers at the school. [...] He knew Latin, German and French, and he was a good musician and the church organist. He was very religiously devoted. [...] Emilio Mulalani featured prominently in the Sacred Heart of Jesus group, not so much as the leader but as the almost holy man amongst them. A very handsome and learned man, he was also extremely humble and pious. [...] Some years later Emilio Mulalani's night-long devotions attracted followers, resulting in a fanatical sect called 'Mutima Utakatifu' on the Copperbelt and Northern and Luapula Provinces, which was subsequently excommunicated by the Church. Short of violence, its later history paralleled that of Lenshina. Nevertheless, Emilio Mulalani earned my confidence and respect as an intellectual, when few existed around me.

The Catholic Church in Wusakile was perhaps the most important social centre in the compound, with daily regular activities [...] since the majority of the residents were from Northern Province, the majority of practising Christians were also Catholics. So most afternoons I was at the church and I served at mass in the morning. A new library [was] set up at the welfare centre, accompanied by a literacy campaign by the Government. Having learnt to write Bemba, I quickly learnt to read and write English. I became obsessed with reading and tried to read every written matter I came across, including newspaper pieces found in the public toilets. I began to spend a lot of time in the Wusakile Welfare Library. I gained the confidence of the librarian, Mr Henry Kapata, so that he exceptionally allowed me to borrow any books I wanted, in return for sitting in for him in the library on Saturdays whilst he was away for a drink.[20]

During this period, although I had my share of escapades with boys of my age group, I spent a lot of time with older boys and men who took serious interest in me. Amongst these was Donatus Nsalamu who had been to Empandeni School in Southern Rhodesia, and was spending a year or two at home before going for teacher training. Some five years older and a foot taller than me, he was an impressive friend from whom I was determined to learn everything he knew. He was the only one in the compound who spoke English with ease and used it daily as a second language. A strictly brought up Catholic, he never tolerated the

---

[20] pp. 78-83.

'Compound ethic'. When the African Mineworkers' Union started [in 1949], they wanted a clerk to keep their books. Donatus, who lived near Mr [Lawrence] Katilungu, was taken on as the first Secretary of the Union. One of the houses in C4, where we now lived, next to the Welfare Hall where the Union Executive meetings were held, was turned into the Union office. I was immediately co-opted as an unpaid clerk assistant to Donatus and I helped with the collection of dues and the registration of members. [...] This office became a popular meeting place, being so close to the Welfare Hall. [...] Through the Union I came to know the trade union leaders, especially Mr Katilungu the President, Mr Kaluwa the Treasurer, and Mr [Robinson] Puta.[21]

My father, despite his lack of money, was prepared to sell everything he had to send me for higher [upper primary] education. To him nothing mattered more. One day he returned from work with a bandaged arm. When I asked him what had happened, he un-bandaged the arm and showed me a wound. He said, "I quarrelled with the white man boss and he stabbed me with a pencil; I could have beaten him dead but he is powerful because he works with the pencil. You too make sure you work with the pencil!"[22]

On the whole every European I knew as a boy treated me well. For example the European newspaper agent was fair with me. When I got to his house early on Thursday mornings, his wife gave me some tea and bread (in the kitchen of course) before I set off to sell the 240 copies of the Northern News or Northern Advertiser. I used to start with the Central Offices where before 7.30am I would put papers on the desks before the Europeans came to work. I collected the money later in the day. [...] I can only remember one racial incident in my youth which really annoyed me. [...] I was selling papers around the Nkana Hotel when a heavy downpour came; to save the newspapers and myself from getting wet I ran under the veranda. Thereupon the whites who were there stood to chase me away. I had to go into the rain to find another shelter, by which time the newspapers and myself were thoroughly soaked. I vowed that under no circumstances would I enter that hotel again; I have not done so, even after Independence.[23]

Musakanya was accepted at Chikuni, the colony's foremost Catholic school, run by Jesuits in the Southern Province. However, after a long journey and a traumatic first day at the school, Musakanya returned to the Copperbelt, and instead enrolled at the local Kitwe Main School.

The year I spent at Kitwe Main School stands out as one of the great hardships I and all the boys from Wusakile endured. The school was seven miles away and

---

[21] pp. 83-84.
[22] p. 86.
[23] pp. 88-89.

classes started at 7.15am. To get there on time we had to leave Wusakile well before 6am. There were classes in the afternoon ending at 4pm and therefore there was no lunch at home for us; there was usually no money for lunch. Therefore, apart from the fatigue of the daily trip, there was daily hunger. [...] I would probably not have withstood a year at Kitwe school had my father, seeing my utter weariness each evening, not bought me a bicycle. It was an enormous sacrifice for him and the other children, but it revolutionised my school attendance routine and gave me a feeling of coming of age.[24]

It was at Kitwe Main that, through Civics classes, I began to learn about the organisation of society and complaints about such, a combination of which I slowly learnt to be politics. The ebullient and indignant manner with which [teacher and subsequent political activist] *Bunda Chisenga expressed himself on these matters was of interest to me then only from the viewpoint that his oratory was at its best [...] Generally, political interest amongst Africans was at this time hanging in the social atmosphere; the Central African Federation was being talked about and African education suddenly became topical.*

One had a feeling that the years 1947-1950 was the Northern Rhodesian African renaissance period. Material development was to be seen everywhere; mines were expanding, attracting many from the rural areas for urban employment. Government and the mines launched new housing programmes. [...] The radio, as Central African Broadcasting Corporation, Lusaka, came into its own. [...] African education was given its first big push by the expansion of upper primary schools and Munali being built. An effective campaign for girls' education was launched, side by side with an adult literacy campaign. On the economic front, there was the introduction of cooperatives, and the Colonial administration began to talk about community and economic development. Politically it was the turning point, the ANC [African National Congress of Northern Rhodesia] *was formed and the African Representative Council became vocal.*[25]

I wasted no time in trying to find another school to go to. "This time" my father said, "as far away as where the Europeans come from, so that you do not run away." He decided to try Kutama in Southern Rhodesia, where he had an old friend who was school Chaplain. He set matters in motion and in early 1949 I received an acceptance for Standard VI, to start in January 1950.[26]

Before starting at Kutama, Musakanya was sent to a Community Service Camp (CSC) in Ndola Rural, which Copperbelt boys attended for manual work in the bush during the long school holidays. He dreaded the prospect, associ-

[24] p. 97.
[25] pp. 100-101.
[26] pp. 101-102

11

ating the camps with hard and meaningless work and the danger of malaria; he rejected all such movements:

> *I despised it as a herd movement, which as such had no intrinsic value […] The uniforms, marching, the songs all dispirited me […] all those ideas of doing good ostensibly, being taught to be obedient and polite for the sake of authority and not mutuality, were totally unacceptable to me […] The uniformity was revolting, and worst of all, I knew that those bigger boys who were patrol leaders were liars and corrupt with girls […] In retrospect, I have a bitter memory of the CSC: the authorities believed that the boys on the Copperbelt were being spoilt by urbanisation; they were becoming cheeky and delinquent, and only temporary rustication and meaningless manual labour would solve this.[27]*

---

[27] pp. 103-106.

2

KUTAMA
1950–53

In 1950, Musakanya began attending Kutama College in then Southern Rhodesia, a Jesuit-established school that had recently been taken over by the Canadian Marist Brothers (Robert Mugabe, the school's first famous alumnus, attended Kutama in the 1930s).[1] Education in Southern Rhodesia was generally assumed to be of a higher standard than in Northern Rhodesia, in part because of the fluent English spoken by many Southern Rhodesians. "*My ambitions and, indeed, those of my father for me to go to a better school had absolutely no financial realism. My father's annual income was £23 10/0. whereas my upkeep at Kutama was to be £26. It was easily the most expensive school for Africans in Southern Rhodesia [...] my father withdrew £5 from his savings. I had to sell the bicycle and seek contributions from my uncles.*"[2] Throughout his time at the school, which he attended between the ages of 18 and 23, Musakanya's continuing education was threatened by the financial burden of fees and expenses.

After the excitement of a three-day journey via Wankie and the cosmopolitan town of Bulawayo, Kutama was a shock: nine miles from the nearest railway siding in the Zimba Native Reserve, the school was a series of dilapidated buildings, with no inside toilets.[3] Musakanya was nevertheless profoundly influenced by his time at the school: "*The five years I spent at Kutama have been a lasting and forming influence on my life to this day to such an extent that I have had a feeling that I hardly learnt much that is really new since then.*"[4] He praises his mostly French-Canadian teachers, drawing attention to their exacting educational standards and aptitude for hard work; he and his children remained in contact with Brother Augustus for many decades. Indeed, Musakanya initially joined the Marists as a junior Brother:

[1] Kutama was also known as St. Francis Xavier College or the Marist Brothers' College.
[2] pp. 108-109.
[3] p. 110-113.
[4] p. 110

I attended all school activities, but in the evenings we had extra religious instructions, intended for introduction into the religious life. Most holidays were spent at the school, working with the Brothers on various school projects. It was during the holidays that the juniors practised living as part of the religious community. […] We spent these quiet holidays at manual work and in often serious philosophical discussions […] we became obsessed with Rousseau, Voltaire, St. Thomas and modern philosophers, whom we read more for self-esteem than for full understanding. […] Kutama was an unusual school, not only for its academic reputation but also for the unique manner in which it was governed. It enjoyed high discipline in the student body, but without the usual prefect system. There were no punishments, corporal or otherwise; no compulsory manual work, although students were individually keen gardeners who provided all the vegetable requirements for the kitchen […] the school was run on the basis of individual responsibility and liberty. You were given the school rules and told that you individually were expected to discipline yourself in the observance […] Those caught misbehaving suffered only the penetrating and disapproving eye of a master or fellow student.[5]

We had a 'Students' City Organization', whereby students elected a 'City Council' elected by a Mayor. There was two weeks of campaigning […] after the elections the Mayor became the students' spokesman to the school authorities and all student affairs, including most rules became the responsibility of the Council. It worked fascinatingly well, until the much hated Inspector for Native Education ordered that the 'experiment' be discontinued.[6]

Kutama's ascetic environment and emphasis on free thinking clearly shaped Musakanya's critical approach to authority.[7] Musakanya nevertheless made few friendships amongst the Southern Rhodesian boys, whom he felt bore an inferiority complex arising from the territory's racist settler colonialism:

The political rumblings and demands for African advancement, the opposition to the European-initiated Central African Federation, which were exercising Africans in the North had not yet permeated amongst Southern Rhodesian Africans […] students at Kutama showed no [such] stirrings. One or two older Northern Rhodesian boys showed some political mien which attracted comment from the school authorities, who were specifically warned against admitting many Northern Rhodesian boys because of their increasing political insolence. In fact, from 1952 onwards, Southern Rhodesia was almost closed to Northern Rhodesian students by government policy […].

Kutama was however an island of relative integration, compared to the

---

[5] pp. 125-127.
[6] pp. 127-128.
[7] p. 116.

segregation at Jesuit schools in Mashonaland. In this environment, Musakanya developed a confidence in relating to his European teachers as equals that would stand him in good stead later in life.

Musakanya was himself increasingly aware of the changing political situation in the run-up to the establishment of the Central African Federation (CAF) in 1953. He subscribed, and occasionally wrote letters to, the *African Weekly*:

In following the events of this period, Kamuzu Banda became our idol because of his articulate opposition to the CAF, and because he was the most educated African on the scene. [...] Events in West Africa began reaching us via the Daily Graphic [a Gold Coast newspaper] *which was now and again sent to us. [...] The sight of a newspaper packed with photographs of black faces, and captions announcing their positions and academic titles [...] was itself exhilarating [...] increasing political advancement and achievement looked as natural* [there] *as it was unthinkable in our parts. Slowly catching the headlines were the exploits of Mau Mau in Kenya which in Central African white opinion was [...] irrefutable evidence of [...] African savagery, disqualifying them from participation in the affairs of any 'civilised' society as existed in the Rhodesias [...] we rationalised it as the only expression of freedom by the unfree.*

3

RETURN TO THE COPPERBELT
1953–58

Musakanya returned to the Copperbelt in 1953, following the death of his sister and the marital break-up of his stepfather and mother (the latter returned to Northern Province). Musakanya found a changed atmosphere; unionised African mineworkers were winning concessions from the mining companies. In addition:

> Politics had come to the Copperbelt with the African National Congress, which in quiet alliance with AMWU [African Mineworkers' Union] protested against the CAF [...] Contrary to the European's assessment that the African opposition would naturally whither away as soon as the CAF became a fact, it increased and spread when it was announced that it would be incorporated in 1953. [...]
>
> The activists were mostly former primary school teachers and clerical civil servants [...] although there was full employment for anyone with a Standard VI certificate, it was mostly in the Government or the mines. Anyone dismissed for one reason or another by these employers was virtually blacklisted [...] the AMWU and the ANC drew their officials and organisers from this pool of 'blacklisted' literate Africans. AMWU, being the only African-controlled high-paying employer, took the best; I found a large number of those who had been my teachers at Wusakile had become full-time secretaries of the AMWU. The ANC could hardly pay anything, so had volunteers subsisting on meagre allowances from subscriptions; but this was better than idling at home.
>
> For teachers, the usual cause for dismissal was woman problems (most schools were missionary controlled), whilst for civil servants it was falsifying government revenue receipts. As politics increased, however, some were dismissed for active participation in politics, as was the case in 1953 when teachers and civil servants joined in the 'Day of Prayer' against the Federation. It is a fact that a little later,

anyone dismissed for whatever cause [...] ascribed it to political victimisation.[1]

Musakanya stayed in Mufulira, where he abandoned any plans for the priesthood, though with no clear idea of the career he would pursue. Lacking the funds for further education, he worked briefly as a pupil teacher. He settled in Chingola in 1954, working as a part-time insurance salesman, but lacked mental stimulation in this 'intellectual desert':

> *In this community I was lost, a stranger and so lonely that I turned to writing daily letters to my friends. Without books, my boredom was unmitigated [...] in the short time of five years I had been effectively alienated from the community [to which I had] belonged; friendships became difficult to hold. [...] The seminary and the all-boys school influence of eschewing female company, and the odd habit of refraining from alcohol, seem to have reduced me to an unbearable 'stuffed shirt'. [...] I must really have been an intolerant, self-righteous [...] spoil-sport.*[2]

He found solace in the parish church, before seeking employment as an electrical apprentice at the mines. Here he ran up against the colour bar:

> *I would be employed at the highest level in their programme of African Advancement, namely Grade 9, for which the basic salary was £26 per month. [...] I was a special and delicate case testing the bona fides of the mines and the Government regarding African Advancement. [...] I had higher basic qualifications than those required to be an apprentice, and higher than those held by most Europeans of my age employed in higher positions. Both the Labour Officer and the Changa Changa did not tell me that by law Africans could not be apprentices.*[3]

Musakanya was instead hired as a Leach Plant Attendant, a supposedly prestigious job only recently opened up for African advancement. Musakanya, however, found the position considerably below his expectations:

> *It was an electrolysis process alright, but not what I wanted as an electrical apprentice: I wanted to climb the poles, be in the power control rooms and see and learn the workings of the conveyor system from the crusher to the weighbridge. That day I worked at the Leach Plant in sullen disappointment, which was aggravated by the older miners, who expressed utter amazement that such a young man had replaced a European to supervise them. [...] The Leach Plant could not have been a worse example of [...] what was 'advancement'. At 4pm I walked home, spiritually exhausted and never the return to the Leach Plant, not even to collect my day's pay.*[4]

---

[1] pp. 133-135.
[2] p. 142.
[3] pp. 145-148.
[4] pp. 148-149

In April, Musakanya secured a position as a Senior African Clerk in the local Boma, or district authority, paying £13.5.0. *"My functions as a Boma Clerk consisted of the collection of Native Tax, writing 'Chitupa' (Identity Certificates), typing for the District Officer, acting as an interpreter and preparing statistics and returns on various subjects."*[5] As the official responsible for issuing licences and passes, Musakanya was in an influential and prestigious position; he became widely known amongst the African population of Chingola. Whilst arranging passes for the visiting South African singing group, the Manhattan Brothers, including their talented young singer, Miriam Makeba. He received his own furnished two-room house along with the job, and he spent his money building up a 'small library'.

> *Some weekends were spent with my former teacher Matthew Mwendapole at the Mine Compound. Mwendapole was then the Secretary for AMWU in Nchanga. He and his wife were like a whip of fresh air to a man trapped in a hole. We discussed current affairs, particularly the ongoing fight by the AMWU against the Balkanisation of their movement by the mine management; for true African advancement against lip service or job fragmentation.*[6]

Musakanya, whose official responsibilities included making subsistence payments to the wives of political detainees, became an acute observer of Copperbelt life. Despite the political unrest, this was a period of unprecedented prosperity and materialism which, in his words, *"brought out the worst in the miners: ostentatious consumption, rampant alcoholic intake and obsession with motor cars".*[7] He decries the *"infantile cupidity* [which] *consumed the mining community. For example, the African Mine Workers Union* [which] *at its zenith of power [...] could pull out its labour for practically any stupid grievance, did not once demand redress for lack of education for their children[...]".*[8]

Musakanya was steadily climbing the promotional ladder of the local civil service, continuing to test thereby the ceiling of African advancement. In 1957, whilst already occupying the highest position available to African civil servants, he was unexpectedly introduced to Secretary of State for the Colonies Sir Alec Douglas-Home, then touring Central Africa, as the 'District Officer'. He effectively occupied this position for three years without official confirmation.[9]

He nevertheless remained frustrated by his lack of real intellectual stimulation. In 1955, he enrolled with the University of South Africa for a corre-

[5] pp. 151-152
[6] p. 156.
[7] p. 164.
[8] p. 165.
[9] p. 168.

spondence degree. Whilst Northern Rhodesia's handful of other undergraduates were studying Law, Education or Medicine, Musakanya elected to study Philosophy and Sociology. At this time, he met Flavia Shikopa, a teacher trainee, to whom he became engaged in 1956. Marrying the following year, Musakanya proved his unconventionality by refusing to engage in customary Bemba marriage ceremonies.

4

EXPERIMENTS IN INTER-RACIAL POLITICS
1958

Shortly after his marriage, Musakanya met Andrew Sardanis, someone who would remain an important colleague and friend for some decades. Sardanis, a Greek Cypriot who had moved to Northern Rhodesia in 1950, was building a transport and retail business in North-West Province and the Copperbelt:

> *Well educated in the classic Greek liberal tradition, Andrew was agile-minded, comprehensive in his analysis of the current social and political situation, and aggressively independent. [...] At the time of our encounter he was building a shop in the African trading area of Chingola which, at my suggestion, he subsequently named 'Mwaiseni' ... there was an affinity of views between us and a similarity in the education we had both pursued. He was as lonely in the white community he lived in as I was in the black one. He discerned the white community with contempt.*[1]

The two men bonded during late night discussions about Ancient Greek philosophy and history. Both men received racist insults for their associations across the colour bar:

> *My spending long evenings at his house in the European area brought epithets of 'Kaffir boy' and anonymous phone calls to Andrew [...] Detractors were quick to allege that Andrew frequented my house in the Location for the purpose of procuring women. [...] We could not help analysing the contradiction and hypocrisy of the time, namely that in the politics of the day, the catchword amongst the whites was 'black and white partnership' and amongst the blacks was freedom from racial discrimination [...] yet both black and white looked with apprehension and disapproval upon any individual relationships.*[2]

Through Sardanis, Musakanya widened his circle of friends to include other

[1] pp. 190-191.
[2] pp. 192-193.

prominent white businessmen of a liberal persuasion, such as Joseph Shaw, and educated Africans on the Copperbelt, including Arthur and Sikota Wina, and Wesley Nyirenda, all later ministers in Zambia's first government.

This was at a time of rising African nationalist militancy. In 1958, the more radical Zambia African National Congress (ZANC, later UNIP) broke from the more moderate ANC led by Harry Nkumbula. As Musakanya describes it, "*ZANC was at the time of the split from ANC an essentially Bemba Party and therefore acquired a large and immediate following on the Copperbelt.*"[3] As a civil servant, Musakanya was officially barred from direct involvement in political parties, though this did not prevent some of his counterparts from such involvement.

Musakanya instead expressed his political beliefs in a more distinctive way – he and Sardanis established a Social and Cultural Club in Chiwempala, the African non-mine township of Chingola, as a further attempt to bridge the racial divide between educated Africans and whites. However, the wide-spread belief that Africans who associated with Europeans were essentially 'Uncle Toms' limited the potential for such initiatives. There was, Musakanya subsequently acknowledged, little room for moderation in a situation in which most whites stood directly in the path of black emancipation: "*the initiative was too late; compromise in race relations and politics was no longer a viable proposition. Africans in particular had taken a position where any move towards 'give and take' was viewed with suspicion of a sell out. This climate was intimidatory to our members [...]*".[4]

Musakanya's hope for a society in which advancement was "*based on free and fair meritorious competition with the black and white nationals alike [...] was obviously a miscalculation because that was not, in fact, the view of either the white or the black power seekers*".[5] Although Musakanya was also swept up in the euphoric mood of African nationalism, he later wrote that in this period:

> *some of the leaders who had travelled* [abroad] *had not only seen that independence was possible [...] they saw prospects of real personal powers and positions impossible for them even under the most liberal colonial Government. As they travelled to independent and self-governing African and other former colonies the budding politicians [...] fully appreciated the spoils lying ahead of them after a political 'struggle'. The imprisonment hazards inevitable in the 'struggle' only served to assure one a position in the [...] new state.*[6]

---

[3] p. 200.
[4] p. 202.
[5] P. 206
[6] P. 207

5

THE COLONIAL CIVIL SERVANT AND CAMBRIDGE 1960–62

The formation of ZANC finally drew Musakanya into the nationalist movement:

> Until then, politics to me were essentially theoretical and impersonal, in that I had no contact with any of the public organizers and office bearers of the ANC who, at least in Chingola, operated at a different level and would, even if I endeavoured to speak to them, not welcome my company for fear of exposure of their limited knowledge and outright lies they involuntarily told their following. ZANC at its formation appealed to the level of the more enlightened at organizational level, and accordingly attracted violence from the ANC grassroots. My involvement [in ZANC] was early although distant, partly because of being a civil servant in the first place, but also my nature in avoiding association with mass opinion or organizations.[1]

Robinson Puta approached Musakanya to help in the drafting of the ZANC constitution. Although the latter shied away from direct engagement in politics, he later repeated this task in helping draft UNIP's constitution. Puta the leading nationalist figure in Chingola, impressed Musakanya:

> It was in the nature of Puta's politics [...] to be a forerunner in political opinion and party formations and later sit back from leadership. He was an epitome of Bemba arrogance and felt struggling for position [to be] below his dignity. He pioneered politics and trade unionism such that at Independence he was by experience the most eligible individual for national leadership.[2]

In March 1959, Musakanya was

> instructed by the District Commissioner to purchase a quantity of food and store

[1] pp. 208-208.
[2] p. 209.

it for the weekend at the Boma. I concluded that there was possibly to be an Emergency (which had already been declared in Nyasaland). [...] I warned Sikota Wina of this possibility, who was of the opinion that as a journalist, he was unlikely to be affected [...] days later, when the Emergency was declared and ZANC banned, he was picked up. [...] That night, District Messengers and police glued onto every door in the compound stickers announcing 'ZANC Aferatu', meaning "ZANC is dead" [...] practically every house owner, instead of removing the sticker, carefully cut off the 'Aferatu', leaving a free advertisement for 'ZANC', which became a household word, even to those who had never heard of the party.

During this initial period of political involvement, Musakanya met many leaders who would become prominent politicians and officials after independence, including Aaron Milner, Emmanuel Kasonde, Humphrey Mulemba, Fines Bulawayo and Jones Nyirongo.[4]

As it became increasingly evident that Northern Rhodesia was on a path to some kind of self-rule, the promotion of Africans to senior civil service posts was accelerated. Musakanya attended training courses alongside older and more subservient clerks from rural Bomas, and was the only one prepared to discuss political topics with the European instructor. He was promoted to a grade generally reserved only for African graduates and moved to Kitwe, with responsibility for the sub-Bomas in the mine townships of Wusakile, where he had grown up, and Mindolo, where he lived:

I was from every point of view apart from blackness an oddity in Mindolo Compound. Contrary to my expectations that in Kitwe I would find company amongst my childhood friends, I found none. We had developed in the years of my absence along divergent routes. Those I met were established as miners like their fathers before them, and we found each other strange in our ways.

After passing the Civil Service Law examination, he served as a local magistrate; passing judgement over former childhood friends, he found that "*there was an indescribable gulf between us. [...] I felt alienated and with an uneasy sense of having betrayed my class*".[6]

Amongst other duties, he was responsible for the resolution of family disputes over the estates of mineworkers who died whilst in service — Musakanya sought to defend the rights of widows against the customary demands of miners' male relatives:

Miners died intestate and, if by accident, a lot of money was involved [...] relatives

[3] pp. 210-211.
[4] p. 212.
[5] pp. 234-235.
[6] p. 241.

descended on the widower to share property according to tribal custom, which usually did not take the widow and children into account. The Boma was the only protection the widow had, and we had to move in and tactfully delay distribution until tempers cooled and most mourners dispersed.[7]

Whilst recognising the value of custom in ensuring social cohesion in rural areas, Musakanya identified their dysfunctional impact in the new urban context and developed his own approach to the distribution of a miner's estate that balanced custom against change.[8] He also sought to challenge the persistent belief in witchcraft and the social disruption which it caused:

It wreaked havoc in the community [...] it was the root cause of constant moves from one section of the compound to another, abrupt resignations and sometimes murders. The conviction and the fear of complainants saddened me, but [...] I identified it as an evil that must be uprooted wherever possible by applying the existing law with some severity. The Witchcraft Ordinance provided an excellent weapon [making it] an offence to name someone a witch or to call or conduct oneself as such or, worse still, to claim to be a witch-finder. [...] My experiences in Kitwe's compounds proved insignificant compared to what I found in rural areas during my later postings. There, I found people to be slaves of their witchcraft beliefs.[9]

In his virtually unique seniority, Musakanya was critical not only of the predictable racism of white officials, but also the ways in which African messengers and clerks used their positions to belittle and degrade those seeking fitupas or licences.[10] The abstemious and ascetic Musakanya felt increasingly estranged from many of his African colleagues, whose drinking was to him a sign of weakness, and whose materialism caused them to live beyond their means, thereby making them beholden to their superiors for advancement and financial support. He continued to find his friends amongst the emergent African intellectual elite, including Elias Chipimo and Justin Zulu, both then attending Salisbury's new University College of Rhodesia and Nyasaland.

In 1960, Congolese independence was rapidly followed by the secession of Katanga, just across the Copperbelt border. A flood of European refugees arrived in Northern Rhodesia, forcing the provincial administration to establish reception centres. Musakanya, excluded from caring for displaced Europeans by his race, was given the task of running the entire district

[7] p. 238.
[8] pp. 239-241.
[9] pp. 243-245.
[10] p 233.

administration in his colleagues' absence. The Belgians he met at Mindolo, who had fled in fear of what they wrongly understood as 'tribal savagery' in Katanga, confirmed Musakanya's contempt for their 'cowardly and mean' administration of the Congo.[11]

At this time Musakanya received his university degree, obtained at the age of 26. This removed the last excusable impediment the colonial administration could place on his promotion to District Officer. He was again frustrated by demands that he gain more practical experience in a rural area; whilst he was clear that the denial of promotion was racially motivated, he nevertheless admits to having been pushy, representing threatening competition to European administrators unused to such African ambition. Looking back, he valued the experience he gained as a result.[12] In 1960, when British Prime Minister Harold MacMillan visited Northern Rhodesia as part of his 'winds of change' tour, Musakanya became District Assistant in Ndola Rural's administrative centre of Mpongwe.[13]

At the end of 1960 however, he was one of the first Africans to be interviewed for promotion to District Officer. Impressing his interviewers with his knowledge of Pasternak and other recent European literature, he was the only one recommended for promotion.[14] However, before this appointment was confirmed, he was sent to attend the Devonshire Overseas Development Course 'A' at Cambridge University in 1961-62.

After a struggle, he persuaded his superiors that his wife should travel with him at government expense; their two children were left with Musakanya's parents-in-law. As he travelled to Northern Province to collect Flavia in mid-1961, Musakanya visited Sion, the headquarters of Alice Lenshina's Lumpa church in Chinsali. Taking photos of the 'magnificent' church in the bush, he was confronted by a crowd of more than one hundred hostile believers, but managed to talk his way out of a potentially dangerous situation. Despite his Catholicism, Musakanya was impressed by the church's achievements:

> *A people otherwise indolent and individualistic were suddenly driven [to] great exertions, brotherhood and solidarity. Properly channelled and [with] sectarian rivalries contained, Lenshina or Lumpa Church had tremendous potential for good. [Regarding] What later happened [...] a large share of responsibility could be laid at the doors of greed of newly found political power which brooks no competition for loyalty of the governed [...].*[15]

11 pp. 251-253.
12 pp. 256-258.
13 pp. 254-259.
14 pp. 261-263.

Musakanya suggests that in her blending of Christian beliefs and Bemba ritual, Lenshina was a pioneer of the Catholic approach after Vatican II.[16]

Mr and Mrs Musakanya arrived in England in September 1961, to a negative experience of British Council hospitality in London. The couple experienced racism in their long search for accommodation in Cambridge and suffered through the cold English winter. Musakanya found himself attending a course on colonial administration just as British colonialism was drawing to a close. Two other Africans, both Tanganyikans, attended the course – both went on to become Tanzanian Cabinet Ministers.[17]

In addition, Musakanya took academic classes in law, economics, agriculture, anthropology and history. He was particularly irritated by Audrey Richards' anthropological study of the Bemba, Land and Diet in Northern Rhodesia and its characterisation of Bemba dietary customs:

> It appeared to be the professional practice of anthropologists that in explaining the actions or habits of the so-called primitive peoples, they termed as 'primitive' those which they did not understand, and as 'borrowed' those which approximated to the anthropologists' own customs. In retaliation, I advertised my own lecture entitled 'The Sexual Habits of the English Tribe'. It was well attended and successful: it was convincingly anthropological.[18]

He was equally unimpressed by his Field Engineering training, failing to understand how measuring a cricket pitch with a theodolite would be of practical use in the African bush. He had a more positive experience in his brief placement with Cambridge County Council's Director of Public Works, whilst his fortnight at a Magistrates Court in south London reminded him that the 'colonial masters' had their fair share of thieves and criminals.[19]

Cambridge University, unsurprisingly, made a favourable impression on Musakanya, a man with a pronounced love of learning; he was however alienated from the wider student population by his age and his colour.[20] After some time, he and Flavia made friends with both researchers and undergraduates. They spent time with an aristocratic family in Buckinghamshire, and Christmas in a working-class terrace in Manchester, where they were warmly welcomed.[21] Musakanya engaged with prominent development economists then providing advice to newly independent African states, including Joan Robinson:

[15] p. 274, insert.
[16] Ibid.
[17] pp. 285-287.
[18] p. 288.
[19] pp. 289-290.
[20] p. 292.
[21] pp.297-301.

Rostow's theory of 'Take-off' was a hit, especially to those of us from developing countries who saw it as the ultimate solution.[22] There was a feeling in the air that this was the era for managed and planned economic development of the erstwhile colonies and those approaching independence.

During the latter part of their stay, the couple visited John Mwanakatwe, Flavia's uncle by marriage, then the Assistant Commissioner for Northern Rhodesia in London (and later Zambia's first Minister of Education). Mwanakatwe encouraged Musakanya to return home to play a full role in the new country's development.

It was during his time at St. Catherine's College that Musakanya was, by all accounts except his own, recruited by the British intelligence services. Unsurprisingly, Musakanya does not mention this in his memoirs, but it seems clear that his subsequent and highly unusual appointment as Consul General in Elizabethville was a reflection of his links to MI6.

---

[22] Citation for Rostow article.

6

TO KATANGA AND BACK
1962-64

Musakanya returned to Northern Rhodesia in 1962, the year in which ZANC's successor, the United National Independence Party (UNIP), first entered the government and the country was placed on an irreversible path to independence. Whilst most Zambians looked forward to independence, Musakanya cynically observed the scramble for positions in the new post-colonial state. He argues that this state, far from being the basis for genuine self-rule, was in reality the 'brainchild and apparatus' of the departing colonial order.[1] As District Officer in the rural district of Isoka, he assisted in the local organisation of the 1962 elections, meeting many UNIP politicians as they came to charm the voters. Musakanya came under increasing pressure to advance his own career, but his disdain for ambition led him to resist such entreaties, despite the promise that if he followed the right path, he could be Chief Justice in five years' time.[2] He instead stuck to the established path of gradual promotion in the civil service.

In September however, Musakanya was seconded to Britain's Consulate General in the Congolese city of Elizabethville (later Lubumbashi) at a particularly interesting time:

> Elizabethville [...] was in turmoil; the war of secession of Katanga which started in 1960 was still going, but more furiously with the UN's final push to unseat [Moise] Tshombe. Tshombe had just escaped but his Gendarmes had taken to the bush, sniping at the UN and molesting the countryside. Elizabethville was unsafe.[3]

Musakanya dealt with senior US diplomatic officials stationed in Elizabethville — he makes allusions to contacts with CIA officials. He was also in

[1] p. 343.
[2] p. 357
[3] p. 360.

contact with Angolan nationalist leader Holden Roberto; Andreas Shipanga, then a prominent leader of SWAPO, the Namibian nationalist organisation, stayed in his house, before he and fellow SWAPO leader Sam Nujoma departed for Dar es Salaam.[4]

Musakanya's later reorganisation of the post-Independence Zambian civil service was influenced by his positive experience of working with efficient and powerful British civil servants, amongst whom *"the [...] intellectuality and naturalness of class were self-evident; they were urbane and cosmopolitan in outlook. More impressive to me from a colony they showed no trace of racialism whatsoever".*[5] He was more negative about his first experience of a post-colonial African state:

> *I saw a wonderful rich country fall to pieces, ravaged by foreigners and its leaders. Ignorant men as leaders whose greed and hunger for purposeless power [made them] puppets of international politics and insensitive to the rape of their country and the rapidly growing misery of their people. [...] The Congo was a frightening forewarning of what might happen in other parts of the continent, all of which was galloping towards Independence.*[6]

When Musakanya first arrived in the Congo, he was inclined to share UNIP's loathing of Tshombe's secessionist movement, linked as he was to the Prime Minister of the CAF, Roy Welensky. It was his year in Elizabethville that changed his mind. Musakanya dealt with Tshombe's ally, the secessionist leader Godefroid Munongo, then the Katangese Minister of the Interior, regarding travel problems between Katanga and Northern Rhodesia:

> *His attitude was that the matter was "not negotiable" [...] as far as himself and the Katangese people were concerned there was no border between NR and Katanga (for him the Congo did not exist) and [...] many Katangese had died for this belief. To him it was not a matter of discussing relationship over the border but that NR and Katanga should be one. He launched into his and Tshombe's proposal for secession which was [...] unification of Mwatiamwa's [Mwata Yamvo's] people and put an end to [their] exploitation by the Bakongo. Then [...] he went into a tirade against UNIP and its leadership who did not understand Tshombe's motives and worked against him. He was particularly bitter against [Simon] Kapwepwe whom he thought, as Bemba, should have been sympathetic to Katangese cause; he did not expect Kaunda to understand [...].*[7]

---

[4] p.383. Shipanga and Nujoma would later lead separate factions of SWAPO, with the former being detained in a Tanzanian prison: Shipanga, A, & Armstrong, S, *In Search of Freedom: the Andreas Shipanga Story*, Ashanti Publishing (Gibraltar, 1989).
[5] p. 370.
[6] p.360 insert.
[7] p. 383.

In early 1964, with the help of the *Union Minière du Haut Katanga* (UMHK) mining company, Musakanya travelled 1,000 miles in the company of US intelligence officials from Lubumbashi to Kapanga, to witness the installation of the Lunda king, the Mwata Yamvo:

> The coronation we attended the following day was full of traditional pomp of ceremony and pageantry. I was particularly well received [as] a Bemba rather than a British representative and had [an] audience with Mwatiamvo who was fluent in Bemba although, to my surprise, I found I could understand Lunda in these parts with ease.[8]

Musakanya also dealt with Evariste Kimba, leader of the *Movement Populaire Africaine* party, and subsequently Prime Minister of the Congo (in 1964). Musakanya was driven to meet Kimba in secret by Deogratias Symba, a young journalist who, fifteen years later, would play a leading role in the 1980 coup plot.[9] He also witnessed Tshombe's triumphant return to Leopoldville in July 1964 as Congo's new Prime Minister:

> I had to see him arrive to believe it; Tshombe was, to my mind, moving into a death trap [...] and would [be] torn apart limb by limb by the Bakongo of Leopoldville who had every reason to hate him. The following day I sat sipping a beer amongst mercenaries on the veranda of the Regina facing the Boulevard Albert [...] watching expectant citizens either standing in groups or going towards the airport. Suddenly there was a motorcade and, sandwiched by it, there was Tshombe standing up in an open vehicle — near-besieged by the crowd — acknowledging the huge welcome before him. As the motorcade progressed, the Boulevard was jammed with jubilant Congolese welcoming him. I saw it but I could not really believe what I saw [...].[10]

Musakanya's interpretation of the Katangese crisis was characteristically distinct from African nationalist orthodoxy. Whilst criticising the Belgians' role in promoting Katangese secession, he rejected the principle that colonially imposed borders should be sacrosanct. He later argued that the Congo lacked any natural unity, suggesting that the people of Katanga were closer culturally to those of Northern Rhodesia than those of other parts of this vast country and that a loose federal structure should have been adopted at independence.[11] Musakanya, albeit from a cosmopolitan liberal perspective,

[8] p. 391.
[9] p. 404, insert.
[10] pp. 404-5. Tshombe's forces defeated the left-wing rebels with the aid of the Katangese gendarmes and French and Belgian mercenaries in the invasion of Stanleyville in November 1964. However, Tshombe was subsequently ousted by Mobutu in 1966, fleeing to Spain. The Katangese gendarmes he commanded initially joined the unified Congolese National Army, but revolted in 1967, with many of them returning to exile in Angola

had some sympathy for redrawing the colonial borders, inline with the older boundaries of the Lunda-Luba empire. This was a powerful cultural idea amongst Lunda and Bemba-speaking leaders on both sides of the border, but one which was denied legitimacy by nationalist politicians because of the overarching imperative of reinforcing the fragile identity of their post-colonial nation-states. Following his return to Northern Rhodesia in August, Musakanya advised UNIP to radically revise its policy with regard to Katanga:

> *Congo was not capable for a long time to come to be a nation state cohesively governed, primarily because of its size and the disparity of the ethnic groupings. Secondly the country totally lacked governing experience in the population; both the administration and politics had been dumped upon the unsuspecting population for anyone to pick and appear to govern. This led to a paradox that the Congo was the easiest country to rule. The population had been used to benevolent colonial despotism and had therefore no notion of political rights.*

> *Katanga [...] was the largest of the provinces, the richest and the most remote from the rest of the Congo physically as well as culturally, and it was only a colonial appendage to the Congo by agreement between the British and the Belgians in the days of the scramble for Africa. In fact Katanga was an economic and commercial venture between these two powers; both powers had almost equal financial stakes in the province which by and large they had treated as distinct from the rest of the Congo. Further, Katanga had a unique mineral importance to the West as whole which could only be safeguarded by maintaining control over the whole chunk [in] the middle of Africa.*

> *Tshombe was right in contending that Katanga['s] place was in the southern sphere of Central Africa either as part of it or independently in it. The fact that Katanga provided revenue to the rest of the country two thousand miles away was more a ground for secession or federal relationship than union. Since Tshombe's [aims] and those of [the] Katangese could not be fulfilled, Zambia's relationship with the Congo should aim at increasing its sphere of influence over Katanga in the interests of economics and trade. Since the Civil War Katanga had become a currency and trade satellite of Northern Rhodesia, that situation had to be improved upon to confirm Katanga as Zambian market.*[12]

Musakanya's advice was, unsurprisingly, rejected by Kaunda and Kapwepwe. Nevertheless, Kaunda dispatched a letter of 'good neighbourliness' to Tshombe on the eve of Zambian independence. Musakanya "*delivered it personally and in a four hour interview which we both enjoyed, Tshombe ended saying 'Tell*

---

[11] p.367-367a.
[12] p. 407-9.

them [Zambia] to take Katanga, we shall make arrangements for revenue so that the Congo cannot suffer'".[13] He later sought to reconcile Zambian Foreign Minister Kapwepwe with Tshombe at the Organisation of African Unity meeting in Nairobi in March 1965, but to little effect. Musakanya was acerbically critical of the 'scandalous' and 'irrational' hostility of African foreign ministers to Tshombe.[14]

---

[13] p. 410.
[14] p. 413.

7

FIRST YEARS OF INDEPENDENCE
1964–67

Following his return to Northern Rhodesia, Musakanya played a leading role in establishing the new Ministry of Foreign Affairs in the months before independence. He sought to select Zambia's new ambassadors from amongst a group trained at Georgetown University in international affairs, including Emmanuel Mwamba, Mark Chona and Elias Chipimo. He found however, that American education made such individuals suspect in the eyes of many senior UNIP leaders, who blocked most such appointments in favour of 'freedom fighters', whose reward for their sacrifices was to be an influential and prosperous position in the post-colonial state:

> As we were finalising the Minister called me into his office in which I found a stranger in most unpresentable apparel, to wit dirty and tattered. I was informed that the individual should be appointed a counsellor and posted specifically to Washington. I was astonished but was prepared to give him a benefit of the doubt. I took him to my office for interview only to find that his incompetence in English alone could not qualify him for the Foreign Service. I reported back to the Minister and told him that the man was not fit from every practical point of view. I was informed that my opinion was quite wrong, what I saw was merely a good cover for the high intelligence activities the Party had trained him for [for] many years. He had to go as instructed. He went, only to prove a disastrous disgrace in Washington. He was withdrawn within six months and never heard of since.
>
> The freedom fighters carried their pre-independence credentials too far and too long into the post independence era to the extent of confusing problems of their own making with the enemy, colonialism, long since vanquished and gone. This freedom fighting syndrome became a major source of our problems with our new staff in the missions right at their establishment.[1]

[1] p. 423-425.

Just after independence, Musakanya accompanied now President Kaunda on his tour to put 'Zambia on the map'. Musakanya found the regal airs of Egyptian leader Nasser 'revolting' but was 'spiritually fortified' by his first visit to the Vatican. In the midst of the post-independence euphoria, he noted the European businessmen flocking around Kaunda. One such contact was Tiny Rowland of Lonrho, who called upon Kaunda during the London stop of the tour:

> *a number of European adventurers and businessmen and brokers made it their studied business to invest money and friendship in African politicians they ascertained would come to power after Independence of their countries. The politicians desperately needed both money and European friends. The former was necessary for them to buy following and votes within their parties and against rivals without being seen to use party funds. European friends helped to internationalise their image at home and abroad. They ended up heavily indebted to such individuals to a point of blackmail. After Independence they presented the bill in terms [of] specially arranged contracts on behalf of client firms.*[2]

Musakanya's relationship with Kaunda was good at this time, but he already noted the latter's emotional tendencies — visiting John F Kennedy's grave, *"President Kaunda did not need much effort to prompt tears before intoning 'Rock of Ages'."*[3] He found Kaunda to be a listener, rather than a substantive contributor, in talks with other leaders. Musakanya concluded that the tour had achieved little because Zambia had no developed foreign policy. He noted the poverty and filth of Cairo and Addis Ababa, was revolted by the lining up of poor people along roadsides to eulogise rulers who did nothing for them and was convinced that such a situation would never arise in Zambia.[4]

Musakanya also observed relations between Kaunda and Kapwepwe (see also Appendix 3) as they travelled to meet Tanzanian leader Julius Nyerere:

> *They were obviously very close friends and had a lot of common personal memories, to which they nostalgically referred particularly as we overflew the Chinsali countryside. [...] They had a story to remember about every anthill, thicket or stream. They laughed to each other's heart's content. But all that, notwithstanding, I observed the distinction between the two men. Kapwepwe had almost reckless self-confidence and unreserved trust in Kaunda, while the latter showed streaks of withdrawal and his laughter now and again rang false or contrived. [...] Kaunda seemed to believe that Kapwepwe had a political clout without which Kaunda could [not] maintain political control [...] so he was anxious to prove to*

[2] p. 444-445.
[3] p. 456.
[4] p. 462.

Kapwepwe that they were sharing [power].

This was more obvious in the presence of Nyerere. [...] Kapwepwe [had] *spent a lot of time in Tangnyika organizing for UNIP [...] and developed a strong personal relationship with Nyerere. [...] It was my first time to meet Nyerere. I found him a compelling logician even if he argued from a grossly misconceived premise. He had* [an] *unassailable influence on his newly elevated colleagues who, besides, suffered from a liability of diminutive education.*[5]

Musakanya was initially appointed as Zambia's first Director of Intelligence, but in April 1965 he was made the first Secretary to the Cabinet and Head of the Civil Service. He had not expected this appointment, but sought to use the post to establish a highly competent but politically neutral civil service along British lines. However,

I was not aware that there were a lot of people both in the Civil Service and outside it who had [...] invested in the change and now expected reward in terms of positions outside the Civil Service criteria. They in fact assumed that at the advent of political change — Independence — they were the public interest.[6]

A major theme of Musakanya's memoirs is this division in the post-colonial state — between the 'apolitical' but essentially Westernised elite group, whose belief in a neutral and competent civil service with enduring expertise stood in complement to an implicitly transitional government; and the political leadership of the ruling United National Independence Party (UNIP), whose mandate to rule flowed, in their minds, not simply from their election to office, but more importantly from their leading role in the liberation of Zambia from colonial rule (see Appendix 4). A few technocrats were appointed to political positions, for example John Mwanakatwe, Minister of Education and later Minister of Finance, but power ultimately lay with those who possessed 'freedom fighter' credentials.[7]

Musakanya's primary task was the establishment of a new civil service. Its task would be developmental, building on the achievements of the late colonial state but going much further in achieving sustainable development. Musakanya did however seek to create a service immune to special pleading and interests. Although he initially established a positive working relationship with President Kaunda, he increasingly clashed with leading politicians over his vision of the post-colonial state. He was, he later admitted, somewhat naïve regarding the realities of political power and the vulgar necessities of patronage and clientelism.

[5] pp. 427-9.
[6] pp. 465-6.
[7] Mwanakatwe's own memoirs provide a limited illustration of these tensions.

Musakayana, himself not a member of the ruling party, observed with distaste the growing tensions within UNIP. Senior political figures were under severe pressure to deliver positions and patronage to their supporters. UNIP leaders were also keen to ensure that the civil service, far from being neutral, should be compliant to the party's demands:

> *Faced with demands for some 'spoils' by their followers the Cabinet must have looked upon the Civil Service with distaste as an obstacle and also as an elite group which was reaping where it did not sow. It developed into an uneasy but inevitably antagonistic coexistence between the Party and the Civil Service. Furthermore since at the time an opposition party ANC existed the professed impartiality of the Civil Service in administration became a sore point to UNIP, who feared that if ANC was not seen by the people as vanquished and had no power to give favours, it could reorganize to give them a serious challenge at the next elections. Regularly I received reports and requests from Ministers that such and such a Civil Servant was ANC and must be dismissed or not promoted. Civil service regulations could not however entertain such requests.*[8]

Some party political advisors suggested that a colonially minded civil service was an impediment to the imperative of rapid economic development. This expressed itself in the promotion by Ministers of 'pet projects' in their home districts or provinces, which were usually found to be 'full of holes' by Musakanya's civil servants.[9] Musakanya thereby succeeded in making himself unpopular amongst each faction of the government and party leadership. Seeking to defend his vision of a civil service which could be both politically independent and obedient to the government of the day, he sought and (initially at least) secured Kaunda's support.

Musakanya nevertheless criticises Kaunda's model of government, particularly the policy of 'tribal balancing'. As well as identifying the under-representation of Central and Southern Provinces (areas of significant ANC support), he also bemoans the effective non-representation of the country's most productive and economically strategic area, the Copperbelt. In his role as Cabinet Secretary, Musakanya witnessed cabinet meetings in which ministers narrowly argued for their areas of origin.[10]

Musakanya attacks not only Cabinet Ministers' lack of education, but also their inexperience in practical work or business. He is particularly critical of the Cabinet's more educated members (seven of 16 members were graduates) who, in order to demonstrate their patriotism, advocated militant positions

---

[8] p. 470.
[9] pp. 472-473.
[10] p. 480.

which could not be practically sustained: *"Above all* [Musakanya concludes] *the first cabinet, aided and abetted by the educated set, created the background of presidential absolutism which became entrenched in the 1973 constitution."*[11] Cabinet members' overriding desire was to avoid displaying any disunity which might be viewed as divisive on tribal or educational lines. However, as Cabinet Secretary Musakanya publicly kept his counsel on such matters.

Musakanya was particularly concerned with the government's apparent failure to turn Zambia's relatively beneficial economic position into sustained development. Writing with the benefit of hindsight, he bemoans the tendency of African countries to blame external forces and Western donors for their fate:

> *Rarely are reasons of our state of backwardness ever sought at home within our midst or attributed to our own actions or omissions. Often no sooner have we denounced those we allege [...] conspire against our progress than we approach them for more development assistance. [...] We fought for our independence on the justification that only ourselves can order our affairs to our best advantage. Independence meant entering the world arena of nations, each with its own interests, some of which would conflict with our own, but that we would rationally secure our own in that arena, at the same time respecting those of others in order for them to respect ours. [...] To shift that responsibility onto 'external' forces each time things go wrong is condemning oneself and the nation to childishness and inferiority complex.*[12]

He is also critical of the failure of African politicians to consider the implementation of the promises they made to electors. He describes the Transitional Development Plan (TDP), instituted in 1963 and still in place in 1965, *"as essentially a listing of expenditures in various sectors supposedly to create infrastructures necessary for "take-off" [...] Decision makers had no vision of what they ultimately wanted the nation to be; they did not discuss what being developed means or ought to mean".*[13] Musakanya is equally sceptical about foreign development experts, describing them as 'power seekers' who flatter gullible African politicians with their schemes, when it is evident that no country has ever developed through a 'Development Plan'.[14] He deplores the use of government ministries to withhold or delay the issuing of licences as a means of increasing the power of officials or elected politicians, thus hampering economic activity.[15] Whilst acknowledging that Rhodesia's 1965 Unilateral Declaration of Inde-

---

[11] p. 490.
[12] pp. 492-494.
[13] p. 499.
[14] p. 500.
[15] p. 503.

pendence (UDI) was a significant problem which threw Zambia's development assumptions off course, Musakanya refuses to accept this as an excuse for the failures he identifies in long-term developmental vision. Indeed, UDI had unintended benefits for Musakanya and his colleagues; the 'war economy' enabled senior civil servants to approve projects in a less bureaucratic manner. Once UDI became 'routine' however, the Cabinet reasserted its authority.

8

DISILLUSIONMENT
1967–68

Musakanya identifies 1967 as *"the year marking the beginning of radicalisation in Zambian politics and administration"*.[1] This was the year when UNIP's internecine conflicts emerged into the open, when Kapwepwe was elected party Vice President in an election that split the party along ethnic lines, a process which culminated in the departure of Kapwepwe and his lieutenants in the breakaway United Progressive Party (UPP) in 1971.[2] The divisions which arose in UNIP reflected competing attempts by ethno-regional alliances to ensure that the limited material gains achieved via the post-colonial state, in the form of appointments and the location of development projects and infrastructure, flowed to particular parts of the country. Musakanya, although a Bemba like all Kapwepwe's leading supporters, had no interest in such politics. In the emerging divisions in UNIP, Eastern and Western Province politicians regarded him as a Bemba opponent, whilst his resistance to the advancement of 'freedom fighters' alienated him from those around Kapwepwe.

In 1967, however, Musakanya was more concerned with the growing influence of the Office of National Development and Planning (ONDP), which used its strategic position in the Office of the President to avoid Cabinet scrutiny of its initiatives. ONDP officials, drawing on a Keynesian model of development economics that was already largely irrelevant in the western world, were critical of what they saw as the Cabinet Office's colonial orientation.[3] Musakanya expressed his unhappiness to Kaunda about this; although the President accepted his viewpoint on many occasions this was,

[1] p. 507.
[2] M. Larmer, '"A Little Bit Like a Volcano" – The United Progressive Party and Resistance to One-Party Rule in Zambia, 1964 – 1980', *International Journal of African Historical Studies*, 39, 1 (2006), pp. 49-83.
[3] p. 508.

Musakanya felt in retrospect, the start of a distancing between the two men:

> *Considering that I really never knew Kaunda before I became his Secretary to the Cabinet and that (which matters in African society) I was much younger than him, my close working relations with him were very cordial. At no time ever did he express disappointment [or] [...] anger, nor show untoward conduct to me [...] he made little contribution to our business discourse, never came up with an idea of how a given problem may be tackled. He was most of the time apparently receptive and read memos carefully on which he marked in the margins "OK, Val", "Go ahead, Val" etc. In doing so he seemed to have had confidence that I would never take advantage of the enormous trust and authority he put into my hands. There was an understanding between us that I handle all administrative issues, at least he should avoid doing so himself, to give him an opportunity whenever necessary to retract. I being a civil servant would not mind to be blamed for wrong doing, providing he himself knew it was done with his consent. In this way I could shield him from unfavourable exposure [...].*
>
> *He hated to be reminded of unpleasant things, especially if it meant to be consistent. [...] Now and again he would decide something quite contrary to what was already settled and agreed and I'd bring up a file to show him so. He would be furious and sometimes he'd keep the file, never to be seen again. [...] He liked flattery and paid well for it. He placed considerable store and confidence in European advisers whoever they may be. [...] He hated being alone and if you have to have a late appointment, that is, in the evening without another appointment following, you are most likely to be kept there very late. [...] He likes to listen to his own voice and vision; he would listen to his own already delivered and recorded speech either on radio or TV with rapt attention as often as it may be repeated.*[4]

Kaunda increasingly operated from State House rather than the Secretariat buildings, leaving Musakanya with few political allies.

Musakanya was directly critical of Kaunda's proclamation of 'Humanism', seeing it as vague and unconvincing as a rallying point for national political mobilisation: "*I asked what sort of humanism he meant – ethnocentricity or medieval theology, academic/literary of medieval scholarship or homocentric of the seventeenth century Europe etc. I must say in retrospect, I sounded arrogant and little did I know that politicians wish to put to their followers a philosophical slogan which neither themselves not the followers understand or can define.*"[5]

Musakanya was similarly critical of proposals for cooperatives, which had failed as a basis for late-colonial rural development in the 1950s. These plans

[4] pp. 511-513.
[5] p. 513.

went ahead anyway; the Credit Organisation of Zambia spent vast sums on unsuccessful cooperative projects in the late 1960s:

> *our Minister of Agriculture* [Elijah Mudenda] *cast himself in role of a 'man of the people' believing that by doling out little sums of money through COZ and Cooperatives he will not only make himself and the Party loved but the 'Peasants' would suddenly shake themselves from ages old village subsistence culture into surplus produce to feed the Nation* [...].[6]

UNIP's agricultural policies were, for Musakanya, incoherent and driven more by patronage than by any coherent approach. Musakanya instead proposed the establishment of Intensive Development Zones along the line of rail:

> *it is a sociological fact that the people always tend to rotate to areas of greater population concentration, so rural to urban concentration could not possibly be stemmed* [...] *we take lands, say, fifty miles on either side of what was then the line of rail, put infrastructure and demarcate it, locate some services and encourage farm settlements. Also do the same in radius of fifty miles of cities and twenty of provincial rural capitals and other medium population areas. Growth would continue outwards and the radius would act as a buffer to job seekers wishing to go to urban areas.*[7]

Musakanya assumed that any successful model of economic development would necessitate migration out of Zambia's most remote rural areas (see Appendices 13 and 14 for elaboration of these proposals). For UNIP politicians whose position rested on their authority to speak for those areas, Musakanya was an 'urbanite' with contempt for the peasantry.[8] Musakanya rejected Africanist models, insisting that colonialism could not be wished away and that Zambia should use Western technology and even culture to reach agreed goals — he pointed to the model of Japan as having succeeded by following such a path. He emphasised the need for early, significant and sustained investment in education, including technical and vocational education.[9]

During this period, Musakanya's longstanding friendship and association with Andrew Sardanis (now the Managing Director of the nationalized industrial and manufacturing business conglomerate Indeco — see Appendix 2) was augmented by a peer group of young technocratic Zambians, employed in senior positions in the government, related state administration, or in the growing 'parastatal' sector that grew with the partial and then more com-

[6] p. 520.
[7] p. 526.
[8] pp. 520-525.
[9] pp. 516-517.

plete nationalization of the economy in the late 1960s and early 1970s. He and many leading lights of this group established an informal lunchtime meeting which became known as the 'Wednesday lunch club' of critical intellectuals.

Musakanya had at Independence originally considered establishing the 'Zambia '64 Foundation', which was to be in his words "*a kind of elite club dedicated to the promotion of highest achievements in national affairs in the arts, learning and others apart from politics*".[10] The foundation, with Musakanya as its Chairman, was createded in 1965 and initially raised substantial funds, establishing its own office and being supported by subscriptions from its members. It initially met regularly at the Lusaka Hotel. Amongst its members were many senior civil servants and prominent Zambian business figures, including Andrew Kashita, Elias Chipimo, Bruce Munyama, Patrick Chisanga, Dunstan Kamana, David Phiri and Edward Shamwana. Whilst the Foundation was not maintained, the lunch group continued to meet informally to exchange information and opinions on political and economic issues. As time went on, its members became increasingly unhappy with the direction of government policy They were particularly critical of the centralization of power in the Presidency, the populist direction of UNIP's public policy and the increasingly authoritarian nature of political life.

In the late 1960s and early 1970s, rising discontent with the failure of the new state to address the vast expectations of the population for social and economic change intensified political competition, particularly within UNIP. The UNIP leadership's solution to such problems was the increasing subordination of the state to the ruling party. The civil service, portrayed as a colonial hangover blocking radical change, was a useful scapegoat for the frustrations of political aims.[11]

Musakanya was disillusioned with his failure to achieve greater acceptance of his ideas and with the direction of economic policy. In 1968 however, he diligently presided over the organisation of Zambia's first post-Independence election. Before the election, he was accidentally informed about Kaunda's plans to reform the civil service. These plans involved the appointment of provincial ministers; the replacement of Cabinet Secretary with a Secretary General to the Government; and the replacement of civil servant District Secretaries with local party officials, directly appointed directly by and accountable to the President. Musakanya, opposed to the entire plan, sought to ensure that his opposition was not viewed as self-interest by tending his resignation.[12] In a document entitled 'Dispersal and Politicisation'

---

[10] p. 608.
[11] p. 528.

(Appendix 9) and in his memoir, he sets out his objections to this process, which was indeed implemented after UNIP's election victory in 1968:

What the administration needed most was better educated personnel and not political propagandists. I was, it is now clear, talking at cross purposes with the President's intention, which was the total politicisation of the administration to ensure Party and his own continuity in power. My motives were to meet political power halfway but ensure the eventual creation and stabilisation of a national administration to serve the people impartially and equally, so the politicians might come and go. To contemplate the latter situation was being hostile to the Party. I was expected to think of UNIP as a permanent institution for all the people and should therefore create an administrative structure such that any change of Government by another party would be impossible or be done only at the peril of great confusion.[13]

---

[12] p. 533.
[13] p. 533.

9

MINISTER OF STATE
1969–70

Musakanya's opposition to the reorganisation of the civil service, and his resignation, was evidently a significant step in his alienation from Kaunda. Following the election, he was not given a significant position in the new civil service. He was however nominated a as a Member of Parliament and accepted the position of Minister of State (deputy minister) for Technical and Vocational Education, a position he took up at the start of 1969. "*I was stunned and annoyed at the* [low] *level of appointment but I could not wish to miss the opportunity to have a hand in education about which I had nagged* [Kaunda] [...] *so much and* [for which] *I had already done some useful preparation.*"[1] This was perceived as a significant demotion, an event celebrated by his detractors and opponents, and deplored by his friends in the Wednesday lunch group.

In his new role, Musakanya energetically pursued the creation of new technical colleges, designed to address Zambia's vast skills gap and to provide practical training and education outside the academic environs of the new University of Zambia. He clearly embraced his new task with purpose and zeal, insisting that conditions for students would be as good as at the University of Zambia. Musakanya invented an automatic nshima maker to be used in the kitchens of the colleges, the delightfully named 'Nshimatic'. He started the youth awareness-raising magazine *Orbit*.[2] Having learned to fly, he regularly visited the construction sites for the new technical colleges in his personal plane; he also established a programme for the training of Zambian pilots.

Throughout this period, Musakanya became increasingly disenchanted with what he regarded as the populist direction of political discourse. As a newly appointed junior minister, he spoke out over what was, at the time, a

[1] p. 538.
[2] p. 557.

significant issue — the wearing of mini-skirts by young Zambian women. In early 1969, young women and girls were physically assaulted by male youths on the streets of Lusaka and other cities, their clothes being torn off or forcibly lengthened with scissors. Whilst some senior politicians railed against the supposed breach of traditional 'African' cultural modesty that the mini-skirts symbolised, Musakanya, in comments to the press and a subsequent letter to Kaunda, dismissed such concerns with learned reference to historical processes of cultural change and a revealing statement of his personal affiliations:

> *I have found out that although I love Zambia so much, I perhaps love a truthful approach more, because only the latter will make her truly free. In this particular controversy I am convinced that the opinion I have expressed is not a minority one as such, but one held by many well-meaning and understanding citizens and, if fully explained, acceptable to our people [...] the views and the highly emotional indignation directed against the 'Mini-Skirts' could be dismissed as ridiculous and a waste of words, but for the fact that the campaign is being waged in the name of "our culture — our way of life" [...].*
>
> *To pronounce that our cultural heritage before the colonial invasion was absolutely glorious is not only a sign of ignorance of human history but public deception which, if successful, could set the nation on the path of irredeemable stagnation [...] the arguments of the militants are spurious [...]. They assert that the 'Mini-Skirts are indecent, violate African culture, and Zambian modesty and sense of values. What is our customary and cultural modesty as regards dress? The truth is that even in my lifetime I have seen my grandmother and her sisters virtually in the nude without this state raising the slightest eye-brow [...]*
>
> *Those who desire that as a public policy that our national dress comes down to the knees or ankles are unfortunately looking at us through the eyes of the colonial era [...]. On their arrival the colonisers and missionaries found our nudity incompatible with their trade and contrary to the religious doctrines preached by the missionaries. Accordingly, they dispensed calico either freely or for little labour [...]. As time went on [...] we copied and accepted the "Bwana's dress. [...] The type of reaction exhibited against the 'Mini-Skirt' [...] is a compound of [the] inferiority complex we ex-colonial people continue to live up against [...] [but] that is not sufficient for uncritically justifying and glorifying the past and demurring our present state of development [...] my thesis is that cultural conservatism is in inverse proportion to economic and technological development; the more culturally intolerant a nation is, the less capable it is to advance.* ³

---

³ Musakanya to His Excellency the President, 'Memorandum on the Dangers of Cultural Conservatives', 2 April 1969. Emphasis in original.

Musakanya went on to provide Kaunda with a historical treatise on the development of 'culture', arguing that the success of the West was rooted in its openness to the cultures of other civilisations and citing great cultures that declined as a result of their resistance to 'foreign' cultures. His analysis, drawing on the Roman Empire, Egypt under the Pharaohs, and the Bolshevik Revolution, is erudite and impressive and an unmistakable argument for cosmopolitanism. America is praised for its 'melting pot' society and an argument is advanced that post-colonial Zambia could draw usefully on elements of Western culture without losing its own. Musakanya praises the urbanised and diverse Copperbelt as Zambia's most advanced province. He suggests that "*The economic and industrial revolution we have embarked upon is in direct conflict with many cherished past ways of life and this will rapidly give rise to the adoption of new modes of behaviour.*" Musakanya's letter concludes, "*it is what happens in the urban areas that will eventually make Zambia*".[4]

Musakanya's outspoken public attack on 'culturalism' further alienated him from many senior Northern Province politicians, who had opposed the appointment of a Bemba MP with no UNIP credentials. His disquiet at the nature of politics stemmed, he admits, from his own distinctive background and attitudes:

> *This led me to believe that it was the order of society to merit your position and succeed working in it before moving forward again. Such self confidence left me no room for jealousy nor a sense [of] subordination to anybody. On the other hand I can in retrospect see that that attitude of mind was in fact a naivety which made me defenceless against, or unaware that there existed, many individuals whose minds burned with ambition for position, status and power and were ruthless in their determination to get it, regardless of the means or who was hurt in the process. [...] My contempt of politics as [it] started to be practiced in Zambia was only matched by my ignorance of its power, how much it could harmfully be abused in [the] wrong hands.*
>
> *Perhaps understandably as [a] colonial civil servant, I believed it was the civil servants who ultimately ruled [...] it just goes to reveal my individualistic upbringing and an education of modern European thought at the expense of what has become to be called "African realities." My experience as Secretary to the Cabinet in the first years of independence was a real disappointment as far as politics was concerned, but somehow I still had a lingering hope that our problems with politicians were teething problems and that the greed exposed was inevitable for people [who had gone] proverbially 'from rags to a king'. I also hoped I could*

4 Musakanya to His Excellency the President, 'Memorandum on the Dangers of Cultural Conservatives', 2 April 1969.

*continue serving as an honourable civil servant as politicians came and went —
[little] knowing [that] African politicians came for good.*[5]

Musakanya embraced his ministerial role, but struggled with the other activities of an MP, including public speaking: "*Crowds have always frightened me and
the sight reduces my respect for human intelligence [...]. My speeches made good sense
but poor rhetoric. It was however not a great achievement to sound sensible in a
chamber [Parliament] where sense was generally absent.*"[6] His fear of 'mob politics' made him wary of the crowds at rallies, and he was contemptuous of the
low intelligence of many of his fellow MPs and Ministers of State.[7] He deplored the lack of effective financial scrutiny: "*On more than four occasions the
Minister who presented and delivered the budget speech had been in office for less
than a month and the printed speech carried the name of the previous minister. [...]
Huge sums of misexpenditure [were] assented to with less interest than a parrot
saying 'Good Morning'.*"[8] Musakanya nevertheless retained some influence; he
claims he suggested Robinson Nabulyato to Kaunda as the new Speaker of
Parliament in 1969. He asserts that Nabulyato succeeded, in the difficult
circumstances of the one-party state, in maintaining the 'respectability' of
parliament, preventing it from becoming a 'megaphone' for UNIP.[9]

Musakanya defied the party whip in opposing the extension of automatic
six-monthly reviews of detentions under the Preservation of Public Security
Act to twelve months; in so doing, he attracted around him a small group of
younger MPs including Moto Nkama and Amock Phiri.[10] "*I suppose after seventeen years of [being] an obedient civil servant, the last four of which consisted in part
of being a speech writer for politicians, the sudden freedom to speak publicly made me
outspoken.*"[11] The degree of his outspokenness during this period can be assessed from his speech to the UNZA Political Association in 1969 (see Appendix 12). ANC opposition leader Harry Nkumbula warned Musakanya, "*You are
competing with Kapwepwe for Bemba leadership, they will make sure you go.*"[12]
Musakanya was by this time profoundly disillusioned with the nature of
post-colonial politics:

*It also dawned on me with sadness that in parliament, and consequently the
country, the independence struggle leaders had changed, if not lost, their roles as
national leaders. They were now privileged leaders or dispensers to a small group*

---

[5] p. 564.
[6] pp. 567-568.
[7] p. 567.
[8] pp. 572-573.
[9] pp. 574-5
[10] p. 568.
[11] p. 543.
[12] Quoted by Musakanya at p. 570.

of followers with them in Parliament, who in turn [had] *a few at the Regional Office to keep happy* [...]. *After* [the] *achievement of independence the common platform was swept from under their feet and, left with all the trappings of power, they were at a loss of how to use it for* [the] *immediate and future good of a nation to be.*[13]

Musakanya gave Kaunda notice that he would leave his ministerial post in 1970. Kaunda, according to Musakanya's account, urged him not to leave politics, suggesting that future high office awaited him. Whilst Musakanya was evidently not entirely immune to such entreaties, he stepped down from Parliament and initially sought appointment in the business world. Despite his criticism of Tiny Rowland, he claims he was about to take up the appointment of Managing Director of Lonrho Zambia in October 1970, when he was persuaded out of taking the post by his friend and 'alter ego', Andrew Sardanis.[14] Instead, Musakanya was appointed Governor of the Bank of Zambia.

[13] p. 571.
[14] p. 582. Ironically, Sardanis later took up a post in Lonrho, although he left this after only a short period following clashes with Rowland: Sardanis, *Africa: Another Side of the Coin,* pp. 255-261

10

GOVERNOR OF THE BANK OF ZAMBIA
1970–72

Although he was not a financial expert, Musakanya quickly identified a major problem with Zambia's foreign exchange reserves, which had declined substantially since independence. The Bank of Zambia was not in control of the country's foreign exchange operations: the government kept its foreign investments outside the Bank's control; the semi-nationalised companies kept their funds in private banks; and Rhodesia, Zambia's ostensible enemy, was using Zambia's exchange laxity to import goods and avoid sanctions. Musakanya sought to raise morale amongst Bank staff, instituting a radical overhaul of systems and improving relations with the commercial banks. He also forced the mining companies to hold their reserves in Zambia, thereby earning considerable foreign exchange (see Appendix 11).[1] Musakanya's memoirs cite a number of other instances in which he prevented foreign exchange transactions that were effectively political favours and which would have negatively impacted on Zambia's financial position.[2]

During this time, Musakanya further developed his critique of both African countries' approach to development and the mechanisms of donors which prevented any possibility of self-sustained productive economic growth:

> The core of the problem is that developing countries suffer a peculiar dilemma: they are catapulted into, and wish to run, a modern post-capitalistic state whose legitimising symbols are free social service — education, health, social security, subsidised housing, foods, transport etc., price control, punitive taxation, workers participation, and state industries — without recognising that their economies are in a pre-capitalistic state of development. [...] They give away free goods and

[1] pp. 589-592.
[2] pp. 615.

> *services which they neither produce nor possess, and bottle up initiatives neces-*
> *sary for higher production and narrow or remove altogether the base for local*
> *currency revenues. The policies frighten away international capital so that for*
> *every venture the state has to find its own foreign exchange. In the circumstances*
> [the] *prescription of the IMF, which often includes* [the] *demand for devaluation,*
> *will become routine, but sustain*[s] *the patient in a state of subconsciousness.*
> *World Bank soft loans will never create a base for a take-off, but adds to foreign*
> *indebtedness which sooner than later will have to be paid.*[3]

Musakanya was particularly critical of international institutions; he regarded his attendance at the International Monetary Fund's 1971 annual meeting as a 'waste of time'. He criticised the subsequent hawking of petrodollar loans to 'stable' Third World countries: "*To world bankers and many Western Governments, an LDC* [Less Developed Country] *is 'stable' if its people are ruled by a repressive undemocratic and corrupt dictator. It would appear that for bankers and Western and Eastern Governments democracy is a bad risk for money in LDCs, particularly African ones.*"[4]

By the end of 1971, Musakanya had done all he thought possible to revital-ise the Bank of Zambia, though he was unable to entirely prevent a further decline in foreign exchange reserves. He claims to have played a decisive role in effectively blocking the 51% nationalisation of Zambia's commercial banks, which had been announced by the President, shortly before Musakanya left office in 1972. Since he had been excluded from the talks over bank nationali-sation, Musakanya loudly opposed the process and boycotted the committee which had been established to negotiate the takeovers. Partly as a result, the process did not go ahead, something which Musakanya believes prevented the financial crisis which hit Zambia in the late 1970s from being an even greater catastrophe.

In 1972, the state-controlled *Zambia Daily Mail* ran an article criticising the Wednesday lunch club. This came amidst the witch hunt of most Bemba speakers in senior positions, following the breakaway of Kapwepwe's UPP and Kaunda's subsequent declaration of the one-party state (see Appendix 9). Distrustful of what he saw as Kapwepwe's Bemba populism, Musakanya claims to have played no part in the UPP (although my own informants suggest he secretly provided funds to the party). Nevertheless, the lunch club was viewed as a worryingly independent association, many of whose mem-bers were also Bemba.

In this febrile political atmosphere, Musakanya submitted a controversial

[3] pp. 600-1.
[4] pp. 605-6.

submission to the Commission established to recommend a new constitution for the proposed one-party state. In this statement, delivered in June 1972, Musakanya offers a further critique of post-colonial political thinking in Africa in general and in Zambia in particular:

> *A claimed justification of our Enquiry is that many-party political systems are not suitable for Africa, but One Party ones [are]. This statement gives a feeling of peculiarity as African — that we are a world apart. Why do we think that we are so peculiar in our problems as Africans [...]. It is probably because this is the easiest way to escape criticism of our actions and failures [...] it is [...] peculiar why we should idolize political mechanics as a special African identity and accept everything else as liable of being copied from the world at large. [...] In the absolute and practical sense, [our] government machinery, economic operations and mobilisation apparatus are non-African and [so] inevitability [is] our political reaction [to them] even if we profess these to be independent and peculiar to ourselves [...].*[5]

Musakanya argues that the problems which had arisen in Zambian politics since independence did not arise from the limitations of the existing Constitution and would therefore not be addressed by its replacement. These included:

> *Implementation of the slogan 'It pays to belong to UNIP', which in its implementation turned Party functionaries into political mercenaries without much sense of national service [...] as soon as some individuals amongst the masses [...] showed an understanding likely to lead to a challenge to the 'leaders' of the people, they [...] were isolated as enemies of the 'people', thus apparently releasing upon them the venom of the people. Through this device, the powers of the Party functionaries were unconstitutionally heightened and a system of hierarchy set in without bearing any relationship to merit, ability, education or true national sympathies.*[6]

Musakanya criticised 'tribal balancing', arguing that it led to the entrenchment of ethnically-based politics at the expense of good government. He argued that no single party can be supreme; the reversal of this state of affairs, hoped for by advocates of the one-party state, would constitute 'the Rape of the State'.[7]

Having offered a defence of the multi-party system, Musakanya offered some specific recommendations for the improvement of the Zambian political system. These included:

---

[5] Musakanya, 'Notes for the Committee of Enquiry into the Establishment of a One Party Participatory Democracy in Zambia', 15 June 1972, p. 4.
[6] Ibid., pp. 7-8.
[7] Ibid., p. 8.

- *the clear separation between political policy-making and government administration, and an independent Head of the Civil Service;*

- *the limitation of Presidential role and powers, and the appointment of a Prime Minister as the Head of Government;*

- *the publication of the records of public service institutions to prevent corruption or bribery;*

- *specific guarantees of civil liberties;*

- *educational qualifications for Members of Parliament.*[8]

Musakanya went on to warn that a one-party state, ostensibly designed to eliminate tribal competition in political life, was actually likely to accentuate it, since local party leaders would nominate candidates as Members of Parliament from their areas, thereby recreating the existing party divisions (ANC, UNIP and UPP) within the single party system.[9]

Perhaps his most controversial recommendations surrounded the Presidency. Musakanya argued that the President should serve for a maximum of two terms of seven years, and that he should either be of indigenous parentage, or 'a third generation citizen'.[10] This recommendation would have had the effect of excluding Kaunda, whose parents were both born in Malawi. Here, the cosmopolitan Musakanya was effectively utilising the 'nativist' arguments put forward by the UPP (and before them the ANC) to exclude the 'foreigner' Kaunda from political office.

It was apparently this recommendation, more than any other, which angered Kaunda. More generally, Musakanya's willingness to offer such a strongly implicit, and at times explicit, criticism of the one-party state and the assumptions that lay behind it, was unusual at a time when many UPP leaders were still imprisoned and free speech was effectively curtailed following the brief but violent period of inter-party competition in 1971-72. The ANC was still offering such criticisms at this time, but Musakanya's statement was distinctive in that it came from such a senior official. It was therefore unlikely to go unpunished. Musakanya was removed from his post as Bank of Zambia Governor within a fortnight of his submission, and offered no further government appointments.

[8] Ibid., pp. 12-17.
[9] Ibid., p. 18.
[10] Ibid., p. 21.

11

GOING IT ALONE, WORKING FOR IBM 1972–78

Musakanya was angered by his dismissal, but determined to prove that he was not dependent on state largesse for his prosperity:

On 26 June 1972 I was for the first time since leaving school unemployed and had no plans for new employment. I was 39 years old and at that age, unless one is in a rush, one does not go round knocking office doors enquiring for employment. Moreover Zambia's employment market was not only small but virtually monopolised by the state of which Kaunda was the Boss, hence the smug "you have bitten the hand that feeds you." The few large companies still outside government control were foreign and all frightened to incur Government's displeasure by employing one publicly denounced by the State. Above all, I had no specific qualification other than [as] a senior administrator whom most international companies could only employ for mercenary motives of influence [rather] than genuine belief in the individual's capacity for efficient contribution. In the circumstances I decided to make no move but rest and contemplate hard.[1]

Musakanya observed with some bitterness that many of his political and business contacts, whom he had regarded as friends, now avoided contact with him.

Soon after his dismissal, Musakanya was approached by the multinational computing company IBM, for a possible appointment as a manager of its operations in southern Africa:

I knew very little about IBM but soon discovered the enormous organisation that it was, and how meticulous and ponderous its employment procedures were. I was first interviewed by the District Personnel Manager, next by an Area Personnel Director from Paris, then by the area manager, also from Paris. [...] A month later

[1] p. 628.

I received my letter of appointment; I could not quarrel with the [salary] *but the final appointment was conditional upon successful completion of courses from basic computer technology, through salesmanship to advanced management in its various aspects.*[2]

Musakanya attended these courses, mainly in Europe, over the next two years. He was impressed by the work ethic of IBM and its workforce, but somewhat intimidated by training alongside younger, highly educated, Americans. He contrasts the rigour and efficiency of IBM accountancy and accountability with the inadequate systems of financial governance he had encountered in Zambia.[3] He eventually became the Managing Director of IBM Zambia, a position he held from 1974 to 1978:

The period from October 1972 to 1977 was [one] *of intense travel for me. I spent at least half each year away from home on courses, conferences and work overseas and in Africa. I had to be in Nairobi at once a month, in Paris at least once every quarter. When Mozambique became independent in July 1975 it came under me and I had to be there at least once a month.* [...] *At first I welcomed this new way of working. Firstly it kept me away from Lusaka* [although] *even during my absence reports* [...] *were being made as to what I would have said at the Lusaka Flying Club.* [...] *I was personally happy to be out of it. It however meant that I considerably lost touch with a lot of goings-on in Zambia* [...].

The travels also gave me the opportunity to see my son, Shula, at school in England regularly. And later my daughter who went there too. In 1977, primarily as a protest against total abolition of the Sixth Form and good boarding facilities [in Zambia], *I had sent my son to an English public school. He returned home every holiday to ensure that he never lost touch. Working for IBM, they not only paid the fees, but could pay for me from wherever I was in Europe to go to spend a weekend with the children in London. Be it as it may, I experienced some of the worst periods of loneliness on these business trips.*

By 1976 I was travel-weary. My bosses appreciated the fact and showed little surprise as I endeavoured to dodge one trip after another. At the same time business was getting problematic, not declining, but the Bank of Zambia could no longer make dollar transfers of computer rental charges regularly. [...] *I was asked to move to Paris in a higher capacity and at most comfortable remuneration. I stalled on this offer because I could not face the prospect of working and living in Paris.* [...] *Finally the assignment was reduced to segments of three months at a time* [...] *and I agreed to start in August 1977. Except my household and myself, all*

[2] p. 638.
[3] pp. 638-641.

*relatives and these friends who knew about the posting to Paris were most anxious
that I accept; some for political reasons, but others for the sheer fact that it was an
important job* [...].[4]

Musakanya's plans were however scuppered by the removal of his passport
by the Zambian government:

I prepared to leave Zambia on 28 July 1977 for my first three months in Paris [...]
*But on 26 July I was called to Aaron Milner's office — then Minister of Home Affairs
— to be told that, on instructions from the President, he had to withdraw my
passport with immediate effect. He did not know the reason, he said. He was sad.
He, as a close friend, knew all my plans as described above.* [...] *When I pressed
him about the reason, he showed me the President's letter which was a mere
directive that he withdraws the passports from me and Bruce Munyama, Moto
Nkama, Amock Phiri, and Vernon Mwaanga* [...] *he had been given verbally a
reason by Kaunda that the persons concerned were known or reputed to speak ill
of the Zambian Government and Kaunda himself during their trips abroad. I was
extremely angry about this move and more so about the allegation.* [...] *I could
never recall voicing criticism against Zambia whilst abroad* [...] *of course I knew
Kaunda enough, and so did Milner, to understand that he had completely different
reasons right or wrong which led him to that action.*[5]

Musakanya eventually chose to resign from IBM; although his memoir ex-
pressess no direct bitterness regarding the withdrawal of his passport, he
clearly perceived the hand of Kaunda in the frustration of his ambitions.
Nevertheless, he acquired the franchise to market IBM products in Zambia,
and optimistically made plans to invest his severance payment in a coffee
plantation in Kasama.[6]

---

[4] pp. 646-649.
[5] pp. 649-651.
[6] p. 653.

12

VIEWS ON THE ONE-PARTY STATE
The late 1970s

Whilst Musakanya was working for IBM, Zambia's economy experienced a
rapid and sustained decline:

*In 1975, [the] effects of international inflation came primarily by Opec's hiking of
price of fuel combined with [the] coming to fruition of Zambia's own bad economic policies and reckless expenditure. Zambia's economy was clearly diving down-
wards and shortages became evident in every sector [...]. Whatever other
problems arose after 1974 merely aggravated the foreign exchange shortage problem. Shortages became increasingly acute. To distract attention of the public from
the reality of the problem Kaunda became almost exclusively involved with the
'Southern African problem' of Zimbabwe's independence, while the party was
harassing traders as responsible for shortages by hoarding. Price controls were
extended, while subsidies proliferated. No attention to farmers' complaints was
entertained, as a result of which many stopped growing enough maize.*

*External debt piled up, but could not solve the Zambians' problems because its
leaders and Kaunda in particular did everything except [curtailing] 'defence' and
political expenditure, which by 1980 had reached 47% of recurrent budget [...].
'Free' education had turned into a nightmare as every January more and more
children were turned away [...] (hardly any new schools had been built since
1967)[...]. Hospitals were running short of drugs and only the cheapest could be
prescribed. Everything pointed to inefficient management of the state and extrav-
agance in the corridors of power.*[1]

With these failures so apparent, politics became dominated by nostalgia for
the certainties of the nationalist movement. Zambia played a leading role in
supporting the liberation struggles of its southern African neighbours, but
some Zambians felt this to be at the expense of their own concerns.

[1] p. 672-3.

Meanwhile, Zambia's one-party state steadily moved to the left; techno-cratic officials were increasingly marginalised by a group of veterans of the liberation struggle, whose power was symbolized by the pro-Soviet UNIP Secretary General Grey Zulu. One significant manifestation of this was the proposal that a path of Marxist-Leninist 'scientific socialism' would be fol-lowed, and that this would be taught in schools. There was a major clash between UNIP and Zambia's Christian churches, which regarded scientific socialism as a form of atheistic government.[2] Musakanya, unsurprisingly, was on the side of the churches, arguing that *"Stampeding for Scientific Socialism is not only meaningless but lends suspicion to the intentions of the leadership. There is neither a proletariat nor a peasantry* [in Zambia]. *There are no social classes in feudal or capitalist terms, except maybe a little 'political class.'"*[3]

Musakanya, a devout Catholic throughout his life, was influenced by the ideas of Catholic social teaching which developed after the Second Vatican Council of 1962-65, and sought to apply them to the Zambian scenario:

In the Christian view, the purpose of all politics, like any other field of human activity, must be the common good and the welfare of the individual. [...] *Al-though the choice and method of government is left to free will, the exercise of power must be within the limits of morality.* [...] *Disinterestedness in* [political] *affairs is neglect of one's obligations to the community.* [...] *The State is never an end in itself and must not usurp all authority over the personal decisions of its citizens* [...] *the ideas governing development have Christian roots. Personal help and the human aspect are encouraged. It is directed more towards improving living conditions and the 'better life' than* [is] *a Marxist concept of production or aggrandisement of the State.*[4]

Zambia's financial crisis occurred in the run-up to the 1978 one-party state elections. Despite UNIP's apparent dominance, there was considerable anxie-ty regarding the readmission of former UPP supporters, who rejoined UNIP after an agreement with Kapwepwe in September 1977. It rapidly became clear that this did not represent any form of reconciliation but rather, it was an attempt by Kapwepwe's supporters to build up their support in UNIP and oust Kaunda as the party's sole presidential candidate. Hasty constitutional changes prevented any such challenge to Kaunda and in late 1978 Kapwepwe's supporters were detained on trumped-up charges and tortured.[5]

---

[2] *Times of Zambia*, 17 September 1979. For an exploration of the wider 'scientific socialism' debate, see M. Hinfelaar, 'Legitimizing Powers: The Political Role of the Roman Catholic Church, 1972-1991', in J.-B. Gewald, M. Hinfelaar and G. Macola (eds.), *One Zambia, Many Histories: Towards a History of Post-Colonial Zambia* (Leiden: Brill, 2008).
[3] Musakanya, 'A Comment on the Debate on Scientific Socialism', p.16.
[4] Musakanya, 'The Christian View on Man and his Place in Society: Principles of Christian Humanism', p. 9.

Musakanya shared the frustration of many of Kapwepwe's supporters, some of who now sought more radical approaches to remove the Kaunda government.

⁵ M. Larmer, "A Little Bit Like a Volcano' — The United Progressive Party and Resistance to One-Party Rule in Zambia, 1964 – 1980', *International Journal of African Historical Studies*, 39, 1 (2006), pp. 49-83.

Illustrations

9. Musakanya, unknown event.

2. Musakanya (far right) with singer James Brown (right) during his tour of Zambia, 1970.

3. Musakanya (background, far left) with President Kaunda (left) and Pope John XXIII (centre) during the 'Zambia on the Map' tour, late 1964.

4. (left) Musakanya, unknown location.

5. (below) Musakanya, unknown event at Lusaka International Airport.

6. In Washington, left to right, Laxon Kaemba and Putteho Ngonda (both Second Secretaries of the Zambian Embassy in the USA), Musakanya and Robert Hampton, US Civil Service Commission. (mid to late 1970s)

7. Musakanya (far right) with Pierce Annfield (standing, middle) and Dominic Mulaisho (sitting, second from left) at the Lusaka Flying Club in 1980 (the year of the coup attempt).

13

EXPLAINING THE COUP ATTEMPT OF 1980

In order to understand Valentine Musakanya's role in subsequent events, it is necessary for the editor to explain in some detail the events leading up to and surrounding the 1980 coup attempt. This is particularly important because the coup attempt is an event dominated by myth, rumour, claim and counter-claim. To be sure, there was indeed a plot to overthrow the government; yet, whether it was ever in a position to succeed is quite another matter. This section will offer some conclusions regarding the origins of the coup plot, as well as an assessment of the extent of Musakanya's specific involvement. What can be safely stated is that in October 1980, Zambia's first attempted coup was pre-empted, days before its implementation, by the arrest of the coup plotters. Government forces launched a dawn raid on a farm in Chilanga, south of Lusaka, killing one man and wounding four. In November 1981, 13 people (four of them Zairians) were publicly charged with involvement in the coup attempt. Air force chief Christopher Kabwe and lawyer Mundia Sikatana gave evidence against the others.

The origins of the coup attempt lay in the late 1970s. Simon Kapwepwe has not previously been publicly linked to the coup attempt; since he was already dead by the time the plot was uncovered, and since evidence of his involvement is largely provided by the plotters themselves, it must be treated with caution. It is suggested that, following the defeat of his constitutional efforts to oust Kaunda in 1978, a frustrated Kapwepwe was persuaded by some of his advisors, including his lawyer Pierce Annfield, that it was necessary to seek other, more direct, ways to achieve political change. Kapwepwe was apparently convinced that Kaunda could be removed peacefully, primarily by industrial action which would bring the government to its knees. Subsequent military action would be secondary to this.[1] However, whilst this initiative was in its early stages, Kapwepwe died, in January 1980. This might have acted as a

[1] Goodwin Mumba interview.

deterrent to the coup plot, but in fact the loss of the cautious Kapwepwe accelerated the efforts of his lieutenants to remove Kaunda.

Musakanya had become close to Kapwepwe in the mid 1970s via Annfield, who also provided legal advice for IBM. From 1978, Kapwepwe regularly visited the Musakanya home in Lusaka to discuss family matters; he was constantly followed by intelligence officers.[2] Musakanya claims that, at Kapwepwe's funeral, elder figures identified him as the natural successor to Kapwepwe as a leader of Zambia's opposition.[3] Musakanya depicts himself as a reluctant actor in any opposition movement; he had nothing to gain except the inheritance of Kapwepwe's mantle of persecution. He however appears to have accepted that it was impossible for a man such as himself to live a life away from political engagement. This was because of state suspicion, surveillance and interference in his activities, but also because he could not bring himself to entirely refrain from criticism of the authorities. At the Lusaka Flying Club, Musakanya discussed Zambia's problems with Annfield, as well as with members of the Wednesday club, including Edward Shamwana, by then a prominent lawyer whom Kaunda was about to appoint Chief Justice.

Musakanya's family suggest he was drawn (partly unwittingly) into a plot initiated by close friends whom he trusted completely.[4] This is in contrast to interviews with actors in the coup, who suggest Musakanya was central to its initial organisation, visiting Europe to secure funds for the operation. It is however consistent with much of the testimony presented in the treason trial. In early 1980, general discussion took place regarding the removal of Kaunda's government at Shamwana's house, apparently involving Musakanya, Shamwana, Annfield, his legal partner Mundia Sikatana, army brigadier Godfrey Miyanda and Air Force chief Christopher Kabwe. Kabwe was to organise the diversion of Kaunda's plane to a base where he would be persuaded to publicly step down. It was envisaged that Shamwana or Musakanya would head the subsequent interim government.

Zimbabwean independence in 1980 appeared to remove much of the external threat against Zambia, thereby legitimising increased criticism of UNIP. As Musakanya puts it: "*As long as the Zimbabwean freedom war raged [...] it provided the obvious dramatic excuse for our [Zambia's] ills. Independence of Zimbabwe [...] removed that supreme excuse [...].*"[5] Zimbabwean independence also led to the departure of Joshua Nkomo's well-armed Zimbabwean nationalist forces, which, Musakanya suggests, had provided a more effective defence of

[2] p. 670.
[3] p. 669.
[4] pp. 631-632 and discussions with the Musakanya family, August 2006.
[5] p. 674.

Kaunda's rule than the relatively weak Zambian armed forces. Three days after Zimbabwean Independence day in April 1980, Elias Chipimo, a friend of Musakanya, publicly declared that one-party states needed to enable the change of leaders, to prevent coups d'état. Kaunda accused Chipimo of participating in a plot to overthrow his government, naming Musakanya and other Wednesday club members in a group that was meeting at the Lusaka Flying Club to remove him from power.[6] Chipimo was forced to resign as Chairman of Standard Bank. Musakanya vehemently denied any such involvement in a letter published in the *Times of Zambia*.[7] It seems extraordinary that, given such a clear warning from Kaunda, the plot nevertheless went ahead.

According to Musakanya, he had indirectly introduced Deogratias Symba, his Katangese contact from the early 1960s (see Chapter 6), to some of the coup plotters. This appears to have led to the idea of using Katangese gendarmes as the main military force in the coup attempt. Following the defeat of the Shaba invasions of Zaire by Angolan-based Katangese fighters in 1977-78, Symba (who was now the gendarmes' political leader) agreed to mobilise them to support the coup attempt; in return, the new Zambian government would provide a rear base for further attacks against the forces of Zairean President Mobutu. Symba worked with Annfield and Sikatana to bring sixty men (some Katangese, some Zambians) to a farm south of Lusaka, recently purchased by Annfield.[8] Another 140 Katangese were kept in reserve. Miyanda, as well as bringing in sections of the Zambian Army to the coup attempt, worked with the army's head of logistics to divert Zimbabwean nationalist weaponry to the farm.[9] Musakanya expresses no prior knowledge of the movement of the gendarmes to the farm or their subsequent training. It seems likely that Musakanya was not actively involved in the plot after Kaunda's public warning of April 1980. This is supported by the reported statement of Mundia Sikatana, Annfield's legal partner, which stated that Musakanya "was the leader" of the plot. Following Kaunda's public accusation, however, Musakanya "developed cold feet and avoided attending meetings".[10]

---

[6] *Times of Zambia*, 23 April 1980.

[7] *Times of Zambia*, 1 May 1980.

[8] Tellingly, Musakanya describes the Chilanga recruits as "...men from the Zambia-Katangese border at Mwinilunga who were legitimately both Zambian and Katangese rather than Zairoise.", p. 678.

[9] Witness Statement, Augustine Mutale, Army Officer, interview 4 November 1980; Witness Statement, Major Yoram Katumu, 18 October 1980; Witness Statement, Major Donald Sakala, 6 November 1980: coup trial documents in the possession of the Musakanya family.

[10] Statement of Herbert Mapili, State House Special Duties officer, 8 October 1981, re Mundia Sikatana interview on 31 October 1980, coup trial documents.

14

INDEPENDENCE DAY ARREST
1980

Following the dawn raid on the Chilanga farm, dozens of leading Zambians were detained. Musakanya describes his arrest, in the early hours of Independence Day:

It was 3 am on 24.10.80. I asked "Who is there?" "Police" the reply came. With my wife by my side and both of us in our sleeping clothes, I opened the door. We were confronted by five policemen, two in plain clothes and three in Paramilitary combat uniform armed with rifles. One in plain clothes, armed with a revolver pointing at me asked: "Are you Musakanya?" I said, "I am". "We have come for you" and with that he pushed himself and the other uniformed men inside the house. In a second, all five men were standing in the hall. The military took up quick positions in the hall and the sitting room. The man with the revolver spoke. "First of all, we have to search the house. We are looking for firearms and documents only. No one in the house should attempt to get out. This property is completely surrounded by armed men."

I did not ask for a search warrant in view of their obvious combat appearance. I said, "Let's start with the bedroom." I led the way upstairs to the bedroom. Two plain clothes and paramilitary came into the bedroom and one, with a gun at the ready, remained on the landing of the first floor [...]. They proceeded with searching, with a gun constantly pointed at me all the time. The search was thorough but orderly and took over two hours [...]. They took away one piece of paper [...] about Honda products sold to the Army i.e. generators, machines and related parts; one Organisation Chart of Zambia Police which I had drawn in 1974 and one 1974 copy of Penthouse magazine. They searched all the bedrooms upstairs.

We then moved to the study. They went through all the books and the papers in the cabinet and desk. In the study, they took six photographs — four of a conference in Ibadan, Nigeria because I was with Colonels in the photographs and two of the Jet fighters I had collected from a Paris Airshow, and two copies of Africa

Confidential. They searched the sitting room, guest room, kitchen, pantry etc..

We were only five in the house: my wife, myself, the twins Kapumpe and Chana, and my sister Anne. I was afraid that the twins would be upset to see me emerge from the bedroom in front of armed men. When we did so, we found Chana awake standing outside their bedroom; he looked frightened but said nothing and remained at a distance throughout the rest of the search.

The leader of the party [...] I later discovered to be Assistant Superintendent Simasiku [...]. He was semi-literate and seemed to think that the number of books lined up in my study was a confirmation of my desire to overthrow the Government of Zambia [...] anything he did not understand was a piece of evidence he wanted to take for whatever he wanted to prove later. [...] The whole team looked scruffy and therefore menacing. Maybe they had spent the whole night waiting in the surrounding bush waiting for the appropriate hour.

We finished searching the house about 08.00 Hours and went outside to search the surrounding buildings and garden. They searched the outside office, the stores, chicken/guinea fowl houses, servants quarters, water pumps, the dam; everything. We finished about 10 am. The leader asked if I had a farm. I said "Yes". He said we should go there [...]. My wife insisted that she follow. It was then that I realised that I was being considered a dangerous criminal because they kept the gun at my bottom. In the car I was guarded by an armed man on either side.

When we got out we found half a dozen more military men and two vehicles. They had been crouching in the orchard and eating our peaches. [...] As they went round the property, my captors were full of amazement at the "servants' quarters" which were far superior to those occupied by constables and the Paras.

We arrived at the farm about 10.30 hours. The leader told everybody not to move around until the search was over. They searched with equal thoroughness both managers' houses, workers' huts, chicken houses, workshops, cupboards and everything that could conceivably conceal something. All this time the leader and one rifleman had their guns by my sides. They finished the search about 12.00 hours.

We drove back to my house. I was feeling hungry but the team leader [...] wanted to go to my office for the search. We got to the office just after 1.00pm. [...] Every file, every scrap of paper, carbon paper, etc. They did not finish until 3pm. They picked:

- a handwritten copy of the "Table of Contents" of my unlikely-to-be-finished book on the Administrative and Constitutional Development of Zambia
- A deck of plain computer input and output cards with several notes on the same book.

The leader spent several minutes on whether or not he should take instruction manuals on Personnel Management because they were boldly entitled

"INSTRUCTIONS" in red, he looked convinced that these were for the "New Government."

[...] We got to Force Headquarters about 3.30pm. The No. 2 [...] said to me, "Mr Musakanya, we have been instructed to detain you." "What for?" I asked. "We do not know, some people will be talking to you in the next few days." He gave the papers to the team leader who signed and handed me a copy. It was a police 28-day detention order [Musakanya was taken to Emmasdale police station]. I had to remain there witnessing the circus of a Zambian police station on a busy night. [...] It was the second day of the curfew which commenced at 6pm and the police being in a holiday mood and under the euphoria of the "aborted coup" were really rough, rounding up everything on two feet after dark.[1]

Musakanya's wife finally tracked him down and brought him food at 7.30pm. She informed him of the arrest of various friends, including Chipimo, Shamwana and Patrick Chisanga.

For October, the 24th was very cold and windy. After my wife left, I had to wait for my arresting officers, sitting on that bench inside the charge office. As time passed, the place filled with curfew breakers or those fearing to go home after curfew time. Now and again a Land Rover would stop and half-a-dozen persons would be pushed headlong into the office and passed into a police cell behind, the door of which never stopped opening and banging as one inmate after another was thrown in [...]. I heard persistent screams of people from the direction of the cell asking for water.

A volley of shots was heard at about 8pm in the area of Garden compound. It was ominous, given the widely publicised news of an attempted coup. Reports began coming in that there had been a huge shoot-out with machine guns and several people had been killed. After a short while, a group of more than 20 men poured into the already jammed office, trying to report what happened. Their spokesman reported, "at 7pm a number of gunshots were heard from a house currently occupied by SWAPO Freedom Fighters [...] we saw one soldier running between the houses and shooting indiscriminately in all directions. He shot into a crowd of children who were playing. When the children ran away one was already shot dead and was lying down. The gunman had run away when we gathered to identify the child, who was a girl." After long haggling for transport, the police went to the scene and returned with the body. The following day, the local press reported that a fugitive gunman had killed a child in Garden Compound.

The bench which I shared with two youths was hard; as the night wore on, it became harder and colder. I could not stand up for fear of the space being taken up by those standing. [...] I felt extremely tired and cold. The constable on duty saw this and appeared embarrassed and pitiful. At 1am, he came and said "Old man, I think you'd be better off if you could sleep in that car near the cell. It is an

---

[1] Valentine Musakanya, 'Independence Day Arrest'.

impounded car and is open. Lock yourself in." I was effusively grateful and moved quickly to my new bedroom. It was a new Datsun and the front passenger seat reclined completely backwards. I fast closed my eyes to sleep but it was cold, very cold. [...] At 6am on 25/10/80, I could no longer pretend to sleep as the activity increased around the cell and the police yard.

The shocking reality that, after all, I had been arrested started to dawn on me. I sat taking it all in until my wife came about 8am. Simasiku came about 10 am, put me in his car and drove me to Lusaka Central Prison on a 28-day detention warrant. For the 16 years I have been in Lusaka and have simply driven past the Prison, I never stopped by and almost consciously avoided seeing anybody in it. 25th October was my first day near it and in it. Quite a different world. I saw at the 'Reception Cells' [Elias] Chipimo, [Patrick] Chisanga, [Christopher] Kabwe and a number of other detainees for other 'offences'. They welcomed me with dismay.... As I crouched on an improvised stool, Chisanga and Chipimo hastened to advise me that it was bad inside the inner prison and that I should insist to be put into the Reception Cells when the duty officer returned to take me inside. "It is much better here, for example we are only seven in my cell", said Chisanga.

I cast my eyes around this comparative luxury. My heart sank. Perspiration broke out [...]. The cells were even smaller than the bathroom in my bedroom at home; flies crawled all over in hundreds of thousands from a headquarters in the toilet and a heap of rubbish in the corner [...]. Cockroaches, huge ones, chased each other in a mad race for mating. The 'kitchen' was an ideal expression of the hell of the catechism — perfectly blacked out by two decades of soot. The bathing room had nothing signifying that name except water gushing continuously from a valveless pipe [...]. The pool of water was mixed with sewer water from the overflowing septic tank immediately behind the wall.

Before I could conclude my survey, a warder came to tell me that I must be inside the main prison [...]. He opened the gate [...] and I was [...] led across to what I was later to learn was the famous cell 15. What I saw shattered my pride [...]. I saw black animals in a pen [similar to] the slave ships I saw in my boyhood films such as Captain Blood [...] over a thousand naked, half naked and battered bodies in an area of 900 square yards. [...] The stench [...] I soon realised was a vapour compound of urine, faeces, rotten kapenta [...] and, above all, injustice!

I was across the arena in the maze of my slave brethren. I was taken to cell No. 15 — the 'VIP' cell of Chimbokaila prison. There I found [Edward] Shamwana, Col Mkandawire, Major Mbulo, Francois Cros, Hans Mol, Kateka, etc, and I was the 23rd inmate in a cell of 5.1m x 5.1m, with two tiny windows plus the squatting toilet stinking to the heavens. I surveyed my new abode. It consisted of 4 two-tier bunks for beds, obviously improvised from scrap iron angles, presumably by some enterprising earlier inmate. The wall was lined with six small bundles of tattered cotton waste which were supposed to be the bedding and covering. The wall was hung with a litter of plastic bags containing the belongings of the inmates. When I passed through reception, they took away my belt and 30 Ngwee I had on me. I had with me only a plastic bag containing some apples — nothing to sleep on or cover myself on a day which was promising to be chilly at night.

I was welcomed by the other detainees with a mixture of surprise, sorrow and some happiness for additional company. "Welcome to Cell 15: please make yourself comfortable (laughter)!" One bundle of the bedding was pushed into the middle of the room for me to sit on. Time went fast as I sat there in the middle of Cell 15 facing the door, watching the animalised inmates of the arena, whilst we chatted speculating about our detention and the reasons thereof. Soon I had to answer the call of nature [...]. I had to walk through the naked inmates, most of whom turned their eyes in our direction, making various comments. Some were saying "That is Musakanya! What is happening outside? It seems no-one is left now!"

Whilst in the cell, now waiting for my wife to bring me food and other necessities, I felt I had lost my self-respect as a black man, and I became bitter and ashamed of my race. We were capable of inflicting the worst degradation upon ourselves.

The Lusaka Central Prison (known as Chimbokaila after the [nickname of the] first white Superintendent) was built in 1935 to accommodate a maximum of 250 prisoners. There have been no extensions since then. They day I arrived, there were 1,063 prisoners. All cells are bare apart from the small rolls of cotton waste passing for blankets. No prisoner was issued a blanket because they had not been available in the Prison for the past two years. So a new prisoner had to depend on either the goodwill of earlier arrivals or his initiative (theft from other prisoners). On that day, as on the other days immediately following, there were between 60 and 80 prisoners in each of the fourteen cells. They were so packed that to turn over all of them had to do so at a signal from the mate sleeping in the corner.

My reverie was disturbed by a call that my wife had brought food and a night bag for me. We put all our food together and had a feast. This was to continue so long as we remained in prison as detainees... After we were locked in, all 24 of us, I wondered how and where I was going to sleep, but I had to push the question to the back of my mind by joining in the nervous jollity and story-telling in the room. The stories centred on how each of us had been picked up the previous night or earlier and the reports that we were connected with the Chilanga Farm incident. The procedures were more or less the same with Shamwana, Colonel Miyanda, Mr Rogers Mubanga, and Mr Maseko of Freedom House. Francois Cros of AFP and Kateka had been picked up earlier and had experienced different procedures, but also in connection with the Chilanga incident.

Amongst the many juveniles in the cell was one Nichel, a coloured boy from Namwala. He was under [Presidential Detention Order] PDO as a 'Mushala Gang' suspect. He was sixteen in 1977 when he was detained. [...] For three years he was in prison, without trial. I was later to discover many more victims of injustice in our country.

Francois Cros was the Central African Correspondent of the AFP. He had been in Central and East Africa for some time, lived with a Kenyan girl, and was a reputed authority on Katangese (Shaba) affairs. Probably as a result, he knew Deo Simba [sic, Symba], who had been arrested in August 1980, allegedly for organising an armed invasion of Zaire. Some of the police who had arrested Simba [...] went to Cros to tell him that his friend needed K1,500 for bail. They took the money for themselves. When he discovered he had been conned and reported the matter to the police, the Chilanga incident happened and Simba was being sought [...]. They conveniently picked up Cros as being involved [...]. The President made fantastic statements about his arrest and complicity.[2]

The crux of the evening was still to come: where to sleep and how? When I asked I was told 'Captain' Nichel would make the necessary arrangements. [...] All the little bundles along the wall were spread on the entire floor of the room [...]. I was warned that the 'blankets' I was given were crawling with lice and I should cover at my own risk. I slept on top in my pyjamas. I tried to shut my mind to what had happened. [...] The presence of my friends was a great help and I also wished to think of the room as not too different from an overcrowded dormitory in the rural areas of the colonial days.

When I arrived I had expected to find [...] Goodwin Mumba who had been picked up a week earlier and allegedly for the same activities for which we were picked. He was not there [...]. I was informed that after days of private interrogation by SB [Special Branch] he had been removed to Kamwala Remand Prison. Many stories were told about him during the few days he had remained at Central Prison. He was haughty, outspoken and addressing the prisoners to the effect that their liberation had at last arrived [...]. Goodwin is a typical specimen [...] of the Bemba aristocracy. The Bemba aristocracy always believe not only in their inherent aristocracy but also in the vocal aggression to make others believe so. Their aristocracy has no foundation in wealth or known education but essentially in being Bemba. Goodwin's belief in this is supported by an outstanding command of the Bemba language. Bemba, I must admit, spoken by an arrogant expert has a mind-boggling and enslaving effect upon those to whom it is directed.

I heard a lot about the tortures perpetrated by the Special Branch during interrogation, and many in the cell who had undergone the treatment exhibited scars on various parts of their anatomy. It sent my blood cold. I consequently enquired whether Mumba had been tortured and was told that, although visibly roughed up and exhausted from long hours of interrogation, he did not appear to have been tortured — maybe afterwards. Mbulo [...] was picked up from his cell at about 8.00am on my second day (26/10) at the prison. During his absence, another

---

[2] *Times of Zambia*, 28 October 1980.

prisoner arrived: Major Mporokoso. I had not met him before but he knew me by sight. Just after lock-up, Mbulo was returned, accompanied by warders and a plain-clothes policeman to pack his belongings. He looked extremely exhausted, puffed in the face and with a hoarse voice. He was whisked out [...]. A week later we heard about him through 'prison telegraph' whispers, that he had been thoroughly tortured and had to be sent to the Annex Hospital for treatment. There was no means to confirm this.

In the days following our arrest, the press was agog with headlines of the events leading to our arrest [...]. Chibesa Kankasa and Fines Bulawayo were busy organizing demonstrations against the plotters. This failed, but some schools were shut. There was bleating and squealing in the press, and condemnation [...]. At his press conference, Kaunda in a euphoric manner added more fuel and said we were to appear before the court in a matter of days. Although we were not this time mentioned by name [...] the message of our guilt was loud and clear. Such was the agitation that there were calls for a tribunal to try the plotters. Had it been in the heydays of UNIP, when they carried the masses, we could have been dragged from the prison to be hanged on Cairo Road. The unpopularity of the government and the Party saved us from this secret desire of Kaunda and the Central Committee gang. The mood of the public, although muted, was overwhelmingly on our side. It silently commanded restraint.

In the meantime the Special Branch and the police, all under Wilted J. Phiri, were sharpening their knives for interrogation to find material to justify Kaunda and the Party's rather premature outbursts. Having announced that the security officials had exchanged fire with mercenaries, killing two and capturing two, they felt they had to find the others who had supposedly escaped. As a result some juveniles were being picked up and being brought to the overcrowded jail.

In the first days the prison was besieged by friends and relatives wanting to see me. They came from the Copperbelt, Kasama and other parts of the country, in addition to Lusaka. My parents came a day after the arrest.

On 31st October Shamwana was taken at 2pm for interrogation [...]. He was not to return until 6pm the following day. He was a moving ghost, eyes puffed from lack of sleep. He could not speak, his mouth and throat were dry and sore. He slumped into the bunk. There was total silence as everyone in the cell visually examined him. He could not even answer my question of "What happened?"

The following morning 02/12/80 at 2.30 pm, plain clothes police came for me [...]. I was pushed into the ambulance (with tinted windows) and driven away to Lilayi Police Training School. When the doors of the ambulance opened at Lilayi, the vehicle was already surrounded by armed paras. I was led to the entrance of the officers' mess building by two of the paras with guns [...] six inches from my back. [...] I entered a large room 20' x 20'. It was plain except for a small rickety table near the wall by which an enormous man sat on a small chair. There was another chair opposite him. He was fumbling with two pieces of paper. As the door shut behind him and me I noticed two Paras, again armed, in the two corners beside the door.

I quickly surveyed the room. I remembered it. I had been there in either 1958 or 1960 in part of the Admin Training Course in the Colonial Government. It was then really cosy and impressive. Now it was stripped, unpainted for years, curtains weather-worn and torn. The ceiling was gaping in several places. The area previously used as the bar counter was barred off with cardboard and I later discovered that the tapes were being monitored there. [...] Also behind the chair along the wall by what was previously a fireplace was a built-in bench. Near it by the corner dangled a string for switching the mikes. This became obvious during the interrogation, since we would not start until someone behind me had pressed the switch.

My interrogator lifted his eyes (as red as a Cobra's) and motioned me to the upright hardboard chair in front of him and under the lamps. [...] A few minutes later three other interrogators entered. [...] As the interrogation opened in earnest (it was to last from 3.30 pm to 5.30 the following day) [the interrogators] most, if not all of whom had Eastern European training in interrogation [...] ignore[d] any subsequent trial and the relevance of their questions to the evidence. They were keen on a confession under pressure; they had a fairly good story about a possible plan for a coup from their earlier interrogations but nothing substantial about my involvement. They were however convinced that I or Shamwana was the mastermind.

The line of questions was:
- about Annfield, why and how did I know him, what did I discuss with him at the [Lusaka Flying] Club, why did I take a trip to Salisbury with him.
- what are his political views, etc.
- Goodwin Mumba and my association with him.
- More important — that I had a meeting at Shamwana's house which I chaired. Present were Shamwana, Annfield, Kabwe, and Mumba, at which we planned a coup, and where I objected that violence should not be used, but that we should kidnap the President.
- that Sikatana was to be present but did not come...
- that the 'plotters had arranged that I [Musakanya] would be President [after the coup] but "Did you know they were going to kill you after?"
- Did I know Deo Simba and how?
- What we I discuss each time we met?

[The questions were] consistently repetitive in order to confuse with the intention to tie me up with the line up of those arrested. [...] Each time they changed the set of interrogators, the leader would make a soliloquy which was more revealing of the interrogator's intentions. The following statements stand *out in my mind: "You think yourself very clever and can govern this country. The day a Bemba governs this country I will commit suicide." [...] "Now that we have got you, you are finished, we will make sure that you are no more the Musakanya people talk so much about." [...] "Money can make people lose their senses, where could you have made so much money in sixteen years of independence? You have been working for CIA because those companies like IBM are just fronts of CIA" [...] as I stood there handcuffed and viewing myself like Christ before Pilate I steeled myself to be totally negative, especially since most of their questions were of a compound nature and therefore incapable of a single reply. The main question and refrain was the alleged meeting at Shamwana's house and what was planned there.*

I still denied because I never attended a "meeting". However, the fact of the situation as I recall was that [...] in February 1980 or maybe early March I had met Shamwana at the Lusaka Golf Club when I was looking for a bottle of wine. [...] Shamwana told me to pass his house and have some over the weekend [...] the next weekend I passed there. I found him within the lounge [...]. Some minutes later Annfield arrived with a bottle [...]. It was at that time I realised that Mumba was there all the time drinking a beer because he greeted Annfield. We opened the bottle and I went to get a glass and returned to the lounge to talk to Shamwana while Annfield and Mumba talked outside about the stupidity of shortages which had led people [...] to be smuggling wine. Mumba said our soldiers are so stupid that they can do nothing about a situation like this. Annfield said [...] 'Do not talk to soldiers like that, they know only violence." At this point I went outside and said, 'I know a way without violence [...] let me just ride with him [Kaunda] in his helicopter and talk to him [...] he would sign the papers ordering change of his government. The conversation rumbled on [...]. Annfield left again to fetch another bottle of wine. Most of this time Shamwana was inside with his mother and Christopher Kabwe was not there. Annfield returned and I drunk one glass of the new bottle and left.

Now the interrogators recalled that some time earlier Sikatana had asked me to a meeting at which he was supposed to be. This could possibly have been the meeting but PA [Pierce Annfield] had not asked me to attend a meeting [...].[3]

It is unclear why Musakanya makes no specific mention of his torture at the hands of his interrogators. Subsequent evidence presented and accepted by the courts demonstrates conclusively that the statement on which his initial conviction rested was extracted by the use of torture and ruled inadmissible as a result.

---

[3] Valentine Musakanya, 'Independence Day Arrest'.

15

THE LEGAL PROCESS
1981–85

It was the statement that resulted from this interrogation, presented to court during the initial treason trial, which secured Musakanya's conviction, along with seven others, in January 1983 (this was despite the fact that Musakanya had refuted the statement during the trial). Seven of these, including Musakanya, were sentenced to death.

In the period preceding the coup trial, Musakanya and his co-accused appealed against their detention on numerous occasions. In 1981, with his lawyer also in detention, Musakanya presented the following appeal to the courts:

> My advocate who handled this case at trial is currently in prison with me, a victim of the same vicious legislation of the Protection [sic, 'Preservation'] of Public Security Regulations (PPSR). In these circumstances I have taken it upon myself to reply to the Attorney General's appeal.
>
> "My qualification to speak before your Lordships is of course that I am the respondent, but in addition, your Lordships will have the opportunity to hear someone, a layman, who is probably the most qualified and experienced in Zambia in the application and administration of PPSR and of the importance of the Article in the Constitution enabling the Executive to declare a State of Emergency. As an administrative civil servant in the Colonial Government it was my duty to help implement the regulations the few times that they were in force. Consequently, I was privy to the limitations and effects. As Secretary to the Cabinet soon after independence, they were under my personal administration, and therefore I know that the declaration of 1964 was strictly according to the Constitutional provisions. I was not responsible for the open-ended extension that was made in 1969 (I was an MP and refused to vote on the Bill). Now, in a truly vicious circle, I am at the

receiving end.

"Detention laws are only found in primitive political systems, that is where the minority [...] or an unpopular government is suppressing the majority in order to remain in power. Thus, it was formalised and refined by the British in the Colonies and handed down at Independence, since more often than not, emergencies existed prior to Independence due to nationalist agitators. [...] Today such legislation and its active application is to be found in the former colonies and Asia, South Africa, and in [...] eastern Europe. The British used it to suppress the uprisings of native peoples, but [...] the Government invest[ed] the declaration of emergency in the Sovereign and ensure[d] that a 'good' reason existed for any declaration, and that it was limited in duration. [...]

"Where a Governor declared a State of Emergency and did not lift it quickly or had it declared precipitately, he was usually sacked or dismissed; such was the fate of Sir Arthur Benson in Northern Rhodesia, and the Governors of Nyasaland, Kenya, Cyprus [...]. A Declaration of Emergency was considered so serious that those who sought to apply it knew that penalties could be applied to them. [...]

"The situation had to be serious enough to justify an emergency. Isolated riots would not be enough. Even a threat to the Government as such would not demand a State of Emergency [...] only a genuine threat to the public. [...] Section 30 therefore is not intended for the Government to continue to preserve itself in power but to protect the public, as the [title] PPSR implies. The point is that the areas where the PPSR are applied are such that every reasonable and informed citizen will have concluded that the security of the state or persons is and will continue to be at risk unless special powers are applied.

"The provision under PPSR that a person detained be given reason thereof within fourteen days is an assumption of how serious the 'situation' is [...]. I said I was involved in some colonial emergencies. The practice was that as soon as people were rounded [up] and 'compounded' the screening process had to take place — even working through the night — releasing some, preparing charges for those to be charged and grounds for those to be detained. A large operation of between 300-500 would be over in a week. Now, where one or even ten persons have been deliberately picked up from their homes, surely the authorities should have grounds or reasons fully assessed even before they start off. If they wait for fourteen days, they are surely not explaining but manufacturing grounds, or incubating witnesses.

"I am detained under a PPSR arising out of a Declaration of 1964 of a situation regarding Lenshina in Chinsali and Lundazi [...]. It is that situation which has been extended to date. How am I related to that situation? I surely am not. If the

AG [Attorney General] *insists that PPSR must apply the Courts must ask him to prove it because if the 'notorious situation' is absent the grounds are vague in their entirety.*

"For your Lordships further information, the spirit behind making use of emergency powers [...] is that of Parliamentary democracy which wishes to ensure liberty even at the risk of anarchy. Such a condition is still preferable to fascism or dictatorship which takes over when such powers become routine as it has turned out in Zambia.

In these Courts statements have been made such as:

'The President may detain anybody'

'The Court cannot go into the truth or otherwise of the grounds of detentions.'

'The fact that the applicant can only say 'no' to the grounds of detention does not mean they are vague.'

'If more detailed [grounds] are required to be given even when the State does not know them, how will the President control persons who are a danger to the public?'

"These and many other statements and in rulings in cases involving PPSR make little sense both in law and in logic, but show that the law being administered has gone astray. It is under this kind of 'rule of law' that, to mention only a few, John Chisata and Co. spent three years in prison when every reasonable person including fire experts know that nobody caused the fire at Chililabombwe, it was an electrical short circuit.[1]

If you want to know what a police state may be, please read Black Government [...]. In part it says, "a police state is where the following conditions apply:

1. *Overruling or short-circuiting of the Legislation or Judiciary.*
2. *Imposition of arbitrary laws by force.*
3. *Denial of the right of opposition to oppose.*
4. *Drastic curtailment of freedom of expressions both written and spoken."*

All these conditions now obtain amongst us and [are] amply recorded in these Courts [...].[2]

In the same period, Musakanya issued a public appeal entitled 'A Call to Reason', challenging his and his fellow detainees' incarceration:

For a year now we have been imprisoned under the Preservation of Public Security Regulations deriving from emergency power which in Zambia has been in existence since our independence. [...] We have joined hundreds of others who similarly

---

[1] In 1978, John Chisaka and other former UPP activists were detained supposedly for their involvement in a fire Chililabombwe nightclub in September 1978 which killed 12 people.

[2] Valentine Musakanya, '1981 Court Statement'. *Black Government?* was a 1960 publication in which Kenneth Kaunda explained the repressive nature of colonial government: see Appendix 8.

have been imprisoned without trial. For those who do not know it, personal liberties enshrined in our Constitution have all this time been suspended to work only at the subjective pleasure of the President.

Before and after we were arrested Kaunda and others have made public statements that we were dissidents, plotters and enemies of the people of Zambia. In contrast, nothing has been heard [...] of our views and what our dissent is all about. We have come to the conclusion that our major offence — even perhaps our betrayal of the people of Zambia — has been our complete silence about the many wrongs — most of them illegal — that have been done in the name of the people of Zambia by a clique that has monopolized ruling power in Zambia for the last eighteen years.

Surely, we alone are not guilty of this silence. There are many others who, so long as they have continued to live comfortably, have thought (hoped?) reason would prevail and Zambia would return to democracy and prosperity. We now know that this cannot happen. Whilst all avenues of expression continue to be closed and the political police consume more money than education for the people, President Kaunda will continue to rule the country like [...] a private property.

We feel, therefore, that since we are already imprisoned we might as well [...] give our innermost views about the political situation in Zambia. We believe [...] in the democracy of the people and not of a minority called One Party; in utmost freedom of the individual — even at the risk of anarchism. Only a nation of free individuals can advance. Any form of democracy is preferable to fascism or electoral dictatorship: the conditions now current in Zambia. Accordingly: a multiparty system and opposition are not only necessary but are inalienable rights of man to enable him to express his views and contribute to his own advancement[...].

No major financial commitments and agreements, including loans, [should] be made without parliamentary confirmation. No modern Government can avoid involvement in the economics of the nation, but we disagree with 'BIG' government i.e. Government taking the largest activity in the economy. To allow free play of individual initiatives, which are more efficient than the State, free enterprise must play a larger role.

The naïve both in Zambia and elsewhere believe that Kaunda is protector of individual liberty and freedom. When Kaunda realised in 1972 that UNIP had become a minority party against the combination of ANC and UPP who together constituted 70% of the electorate, he then decided, contrary to his previous pledges to the people of Zambia to turn UNIP into the only legal party. But the One Party Constitution was overwhelmingly rejected when less than 40% of the electorate turned up to vote in the 1973 elections.

74

The One Party System as it is today is not in the interests of unity but is designed to keep Kaunda and his cohorts in power for all times. Zambians are more united perhaps than any newly independent African country and they do not need a dictatorship to enforce unity. In any case in diversity there is greater strength.

[...] the expenditure on political police (SB) has increased fourfold, while no new schools have been built since 1973. The biggest and most expensive government building built since independence is the Headquarters of Special Branch in Lusaka [...].

For Kaunda to keep himself in power he surrounds himself with illiterates and semi-educated literates. Those he claims to be educated are always of the 'burnt out' species, always abounding in potential but never in performance. Consequently the Kaunda Government has been incapable of solving a single major problem facing the nation. Instead his ministers and [Members of the Central Committee MCCs] *go round the country urging people to solve problems which they (the Government) alone can solve because they have the authority and means.*

The best people in the land are either not used or misused. Most of the things we inherited at independence in wonderful working order have been wrecked ... all information media are now controlled by the President. He appoints and fires Editors and Directors. The country is completely shut off from the truth and gets no news except that directed and controlled by the President. [...]

The economic measures taken in the names of nationalisation [were] *less for national benefit than to increase* [Kaunda's] *personal power — as they increase areas to which he can appoint stooges — which he hopes will enable him to bring unions under control. For example, what specifically have miners gained since takeover? Nothing — in fact as workers they have lost out.*

[...] unlike other insincere critics who say Zambia would enjoy orderly progress if it were not for the wrong advisors who surround President Kaunda, we say it is Kaunda himself who is the problem. He must leave the presidency for the necessary reforms to be made and to work. He has outlived his usefulness and is no longer capable of providing a positive solution to a single problem [...].

Musakanya and the others convicted appealed to the Supreme Court in 1984. He and three others were acquitted in April 1985. Although the state denied that any of those convicted had been tortured at Lilayi, the Supreme Court found that the statement on which Musakanya's conviction rested had been extracted by the use of torture.

16

EPILOGUE: LIFE AFTER DEATH ROW
1985–94[1]

Valentine Musakanya was released from prison in 1985. Many of his friends, including Edward Shamwana, remained on death row until they received a Presidential pardon in 1990. Unsurprisingly, Musakanya was profoundly changed, physically and emotionally, by his incarceration and the threat of execution which had hung over him. Whereas he had previously been an open and trusting person, he was now suspicious and highly critical of those who came seeking his advice. In the late 1980s, he was often present at the family-controlled Honda franchise run mainly by his sons at the North end of Cairo Road in Lusaka, but he took little active part in business affairs. He considered settling on the land he owned in Kasama but, following his mother's death in 1992, he lost interest in returning to the Northern Province.

Unlike Edward Shamwana, Musakanya played only a minor role in the Movement for Multi-party Democracy (MMD) when it was launched in 1990. He was critical of what he saw as the party leadership's lack of vision for government, believing it was only united insofar as removing Kaunda from power was concerned. He was intolerant of the many senior politicians who now sought his advice and support. He sought to dissuade Shamwana from challenging Chiluba for the MMD leadership. Musakanya did however speak at some MMD rallies, for example in Ndola.

Following the MMD's election in 1991, Musakanya briefly served as a consultant advising Chiluba on the reorganisation of the civil service for the multi-party Third Republic. Briefly, he sought to implement his longstanding recommendations on how a post-colonial civil service should be organised, to serve the people and not the ruling party (see Appendices 1 and 9). His advice was however not heeded — he felt insulted at being kept waiting for hours by

---

[1] This section draws on interviews with Musakanya's family members and close friends, August 2006.

Chiluba in the corridors of State House.

Valentine Musakanya's health never entirely recovered from his period in detention. He suffered from respiratory problems in the last years of his life, and died in March 1994, aged 63.

APPENDICES

Musakanya's Writings

This section provides extracts from some of Musakanya's most important writings on important themes related to Zambia's post-colonial political and economic development. In these various documents, most undated, he elaborates on some of the key themes touched on above.

Appendix 1
What Makes a Good Civil Servant?

From 'The Working of the Civil Service in a Parliamentary Democratic Cabinet'

We could summarise what qualities, qualifications and combinations thereof which are to be looked for in an ideal top civil servant heading a ministry:

1. Education: He should be a truly educated person and not merely certified. There are, in contrast to what I mean, many educated illiterates [...]. He should be widely read and acquainted with major disciplines of thought. It is in this regard that 'liberal' education is preferred to sciences. Perhaps the reason is although men work by sciences and technology they live and think by the arts. His education should be continuous through sustained reading and intellectual explanations. Simply, he should be a self-motivated thinker.

2. Leadership: He should provide leadership of his ministry through capacity for anticipating problems and providing long-term solutions by thorough planning. Leadership is not possible without capacity for decision-making. A good Permanent Secretary (PS) should be a quick but precise decision-maker. Apart from unexplored policy issues, his desk must be where the buck ends. His subordinates must be confident when approaching him with a problem that they will return with an answer.

3. Delegation: He should delegate clearly and generously. His subordinates and departmental heads should know clearly their areas of responsibility, particularly as regards their powers of decision-making. They should be made to do the job they are paid and appointed for.

4. Knowledge of the Law: It is incumbent upon every PS to know the law, not only relating to the portfolio he is administering but as much as possible for the whole administration.

It goes without saying that a Senior Civil Servant (CS) like a PS should know the country like the back of his hand in all aspects — socially, economically and geographically. Although he must in my opinion leave politics to the politicians, he should be well aware of its currents and the administrative inputs necessarily resulting. Recently we have had a sad situation whereby those directing ministries know little about the country. They left school or University, joined the CS in Lusaka and became PS without having seen or worked in other parts of the country. In 1967 we had a PS, Mines, who had never been to the Copperbelt and had never seen a copper wirebar although he dished out monthly production statistics.

5. Economics and Finance: PS's responsibility does not end with being the accounting officer. Anybody occupying this position should foremost be cost conscious and be aware of his own Ministry's contribution to revenue. [...] There should be economy throughout the operation — both in words and on paper! He is expected to know Government financial procedures well to be able to budget for his ministry properly and avoid the distortions to the national economy that result from unusually high supplementaries. [...] it is highly desirable for senior officers to pass an appropriate examination in applied economics and public finance.

6. Sense of History: From knowledge of the law and country there should flow a sense of history. A senior official's functions should have value beyond his time and where possible should draw upon the past. He is working in history and he is recording history. Files and other forms of record are not there for the convenience of putting away unpleasant issues but to provide a reference for the future and probably a correction or an improvement on the past interpretation of the same issues.

In brief the ideal Civil Servant should be a man of solid, all-round intellectual capacity who continues to keep himself abreast with the current voluminous general knowledge and find its place in history, past and future.

Appendix 2
Economic Reform, INDECO and UDI

From V. Musakanya, 'Economic Reforms' [In discussions with President Kaunda during the 'Zambia on the Map' tour of 1964, see Chapter 7]

I raised the subject of state participation in industry, explaining its inevitability in a developing country. [...] I clearly stated the likely pitfalls and successes. For a success story I mentioned IRI [*Istituto per la Ricostruzione Industriale*, Institute for Industrial Reconstruction] of Italy, a country we had visited two weeks earlier. I said that Indeco (then little known, but the only Government-owned commercial and financing concern) could be a vehicle for Government participation. I ended with a caution that, for Indeco to be as successful as IRI, it should be free from [political] involvement. Therefore the price will be the existence of three independent powerful people in the country: namely the President of Zambia, the Governor of the Central Bank and the Managing Director of Indeco.

The President welcomed the idea, but wondered who would be the right person to manage an Indeco with a new mandate as proposed. I suggested Andrew Sardanis. He enthusiastically accepted the suggestion. [...] On 1/4/65 I was appointed Secretary to the Cabinet and I worked [reported] directly to [Kaunda] with an adjoining door between us. Before I could remind him of the Dublin conversation, I intercepted a letter in his Secretary's office appointing as Managing Director of Indeco someone other than Sardanis. I took it back to him. He agreed to change the appointment to Sardanis. This was the beginning of Government's involvement in business, which earlier than expected would pervade the entire economy — in most areas for the better, in some areas for the worse. It also marked the creation of opportunities for private Zambians to enter business on a viable scale.

Indeco had been formed in 1960 by the Northern Rhodesia Government to promote industrial and commercial development. Indeco and its counterpart, the Land Bank, were in practice institutions for assisting Europeans only, since the securities required by these institutions were deliberately beyond the capacity of Africans. For example, few Africans held land titles; their holding was according to customary law. Due to economic discrimination, none could meet the capital requirements. To circumvent these obstacles, the UNIP Government had in 1964 created the Credit Organization of Zambia (COZ) to give agricultural loans [...]. Security requirements were almost waived and COZ gave a large number of loans. As was to be expected of political loans, COZ yielded no agricultural miracle and folded some five years later with massive losses.

Until Sardanis took over Indeco, it had been conservatively managed [...]. Sardanis' mandate was to expand the role of Indeco and thereby increase the Zambian presence in business and industry by direct investment in both new and existing ventures, and by extending industrial loans to Zambians whom Indeco would, if necessary, help with management. He rapidly expanded the minute organization he found, initiated studies for various projects, and boosted loans to Zambians to more than 50% of all the loans granted. Whilst the direct investment projects held a lot of promise, the outcome of the loans to Zambians soon looked doubtful. [...] Nevertheless, the experienced gained by young Zambians whom Sardanis recruited to Indeco at that time was in later years to contribute to the nucleus of Zambian entrepreneurship. [...] Sardanis's gift to learn fast, combined with a formidable capacity for figures, made Indeco a fair substitute for our lack of experience in what was the Ministry of Commerce and Industry. Sardanis also had a further advantage in my position as Secretary to the Cabinet. We cut the red tape.

We cannot usefully speculate on [how Indeco might have developed] if UDI [Rhodesia's Unilateral Declaration of Independence] had not intervened. [...] UDI thrust heavy responsibilities on Indeco, thereby drawing it into the arena of Government operations and political forces. The first big UDI responsibility which fell to Indeco in November 1965 was haulage between Zambia and Tanzania. In contingency planning against UDI, one of the problems was transport routes. What would Zambia do if Rhodesia cut off the railway route to the South? There was the Benguela Railway, but it would not be enough.... Andrew Kashita and I went several times to London between August and October [1965] to ask the British Government [...] for help to prepare for the consequences. One of our plans was a large road haulage operation between Kapiri Mposhi and Dar es Salaam, while the possibility of a rail link was being sounded out at higher level. The attitude of the British officials was discouraging, it not at times contemptuous. We were told that the UTC, who ran Central African Road Services (CARS) in Zambia and in East Africa, claimed that the Great North Road was not capable of bearing 300 tons of heavy traffic per month and the road would not withstand it for six months. We were informed that UTC (or any other British company) would [not] be interested in such a foolhardy venture. [...] In reply to President Kaunda's request to Britain to assist in building a Zambia/Tanzania pipeline using the army engineering corps, Mr [Harold] Wilson replied that it would cost £34m and take 5 years.

The British attitude puzzled me, perhaps because I was naïve enough not to believe that any sympathies they could have for Rhodesian 'Kith and Kin' could so pathetically blind them to their future interests. The new Government of Zambia had almost blind faith in the British sense of justice and thought it had goodwill to Zambia to the extent that it was almost natural for Zambia to approach the British first with a new business proposal. [...] It would appear that during that period of rapid decolonization, Britain acquired into its system a poisonous psyche from the returning flood of colonial settlers and administrators who were embittered against the former colonies and, because of their absence from Europe, were ignorant of the changed economically competitive environment of Europe. Thus, whilst Britain shed the colonial empire, it retained hold of the imperial mind.

It was during these desperate days that a memory of 1962 recurred. In June 1962 I drove on the motorway between Turin and Venice and all the way I saw a fleet of trucks taking export goods from the industrial North to Venice and Trieste. I asked the Italian Charge D'Affaires Mr Balbini to come to my office. I discussed the transport problem with him [...] a few days later Mr Tito [surname unclear] of Intersomer arrived. I put him in touch with Sardanis. In a matter of days they agreed on the formation on Zamtan. President Kaunda phoned President Nyerere who agreed [...] six months after the first contract, Zamtan trucks were plying between Lusaka and Dar es Salaam. [...] Having suffered frustration and humiliation in our begging negotiations with Britain, I lent a lot of weight to ventures with Italian companies. Thus they got the pipeline contract and executed it in half the time at half the cost. We contracted Zambian Airways with them and it flew the following day, even without route maps and log books, which were being held in Salisbury. The Italian role in our survival of UDI needs more thanks than a long write-up or the money paid for services rendered can demonstrate.

By 1966, Indeco stood out as the best economic success story since Independence, and this despite the sabotage of UDI. It was Indeco that created actual new jobs when the mines were pulling back and the Government was creating political and ultimately inflationary jobs. It has been a pattern with Zambian politicians, led by the President, to destroy any institution, whether government or parastatal, that shows signs of success and competence. [...] Accordingly, Indeco and Sardanis came into political focus. Sardanis was feted for friendship by all politicians; those not doing so were busy elsewhere lobbying enemies. State House became a sitting-room for Kaunda to acquire the perfume of success and ensure that his rivals did not wear it. [...] In recognition, Sardanis was appointed Permanent Secretary in the Ministry of Commerce and Industry (later Minister of State for Participation) and also Permanent Secretary, Ministry of Finance, in addition to being Chairman of Indeco. In view of the political cloud which began building from mid-1966 and was to continue until 1971, there was no better vehicle for Kaunda to ride in order to boost his popularity; Sardanis would be his personal driver.

Appendix 3
Kaunda and Kapwepwe

From 'Influences on Kaunda'

[Through his education and upbringing, Kaunda] became the surrogate of the Church of Scotland and the Protestant missionaries as a whole. His family [...] was a missionary plant in the midst of the Bemba. [...] His father died when he was eight and his mother had no possessions. [...] the Missionaries at Lubwa pushed him along [...] but that was only so far as education was concerned. They could not establish his roots into the Bemba community. They were still regarded as foreigners and throughout his childhood, he believed he would one day return to Nyasaland. [...] After his father's death the insecurity increased and could only be overcome by local friendship [...] the influences of Kapwepwe, [Malama] Sokoni and [Kapasa] Makasa on Kaunda. The family's continued stay in Chinsali depended on these relationships and friendships.

Kaunda met Kapwepwe in 1934, the latter two years older. Neither lived in the village; their families were 'migrant' workers at the European mission stations. [...] Kapwepwe and Sokoni, for no fault of theirs, had to start school late and at a lower level. [...] For Kaunda they provided security and testimonials of being a Chinsali boy. This became more necessary as they moved from Chinsali into the urban wilds. Kapwepwe and Sokoni had relatives and friends in these areas from extended families from Northern and Luapula Provinces. [...] Kaunda did not relate, he only related through Kapwepwe, Sokoni or Makasa, and it was through these relationships that he was to broaden his base, first amongst those from Northern and Luapula Provinces and later on the line of rail where he met Changufu, Chimba, Chileshe, Nkonde, etc. It was only with them that later they would [be able to] challenge Nkumbula and break away to form ZANC.

Whereas in Northern Province they were a Chinsali clique which considered itself an educated elite [...] on the Copperbelt they impressed nobody with their [limited] education, but had relatives and the Bemba language. This helped them establish a following which Nkumbula could not permanently hold. [...] Whatever Kaunda did in 'warming up Chinsali' as a provincial organizer could not have stuck without Kapwepwe. Equally on the Copperbelt, it was Kapwepwe who had to introduce Kaunda, and as the organization grew, only the shadow of Kapwepwe could prevent Kaunda being ousted as a Nyasalander. For the other tribes to kick out Kaunda would mean Kapwepwe taking over, and they feared his 'extremism' and following. [...] The Bembas wished Kapwepwe to take up leadership, but he was all too aware of the need for unity which could be endangered by such a move at that crucial time, and [he] had [...] confidence in Kaunda to follow his advice. Only Katilungu did not go along with this, and kept the Unions as long as possible away from UNIP. Thus, the fight for the Copperbelt following was not between Kapwepwe and Kaunda [...] but between Kapwepwe and Katilungu and Robinson Puta. There is no doubt in my mind that had Katilungu lived, Kaunda's leadership could have been short-lived and the chances were that the ANC would have been the first Zambian Government.[1]

Kapwepwe had [a] complex character [...]. It could only be understood by understanding the Chinsali character of stubbornness and single-minded commitment. [...] With the tragic death of Katilungu in 1961, Kapwepwe dominated Bemba politics; his only living rival Robinson Puta was too fully absorbed in business to engage in full-time politics.

How is it that two persons so ideologically different — Kapwepwe, an agnostic and Kaunda, a Calvinistic Christian — remained such close friends? It stemmed from small village sentiments and further, that as they moved away from home at a rather late age, they needed each other's protection from the urbanites, whom they neither understood not trusted at the beginning. [...] It is very difficult today, with the very rapid transport available in Zambia, to visualise the gap that existed in the 1940s between the outlooks of town and rural dwellers. [...] The Chinsali clique had gone to the Copperbelt aping what they thought were civilised white attitudes, only to find that the Copperbelt laughed at them.

In elected politics everybody must have a base [...]. That base can be a village, a tribe, a specific opinion. Kaunda did not have any of these at the beginning; his base was Kapwepwe. [...] When Kapwepwe returned from India, the British either knew or suspected his political associations. [He] seemed to have been under the influence of Nehru, whom they thought had carried the British socialism of his English schooldays too far. With the early [post-colonial] experiences they were having with Nkrumah, they were not happy with him. Furthermore, with Britain heavily dependent on the USA after the war,

---

[1] Katilungu served briefly as Acting National President of the ANC in 1961.

which was pushing her to shed the empire in order to forestall international communism, they could not allow a communist suspect to assume power. [...] So Kaunda was convenient, a vouched protestant and a teetotaller, which suited the McCarthy era. [...] Kaunda's activities from this time onwards became focused on 'image construction' for himself [...] his overseas visits became more frequent whilst Kapwepwe remained behind to keep unity of the Party. [...] By making personal contacts abroad, including with the Colonial Office and the Church of Scotland, he was being appraised of progress in the British Government's thinking, even its timetable [for decolonisation]. Groups in the USA and the UK put up good PR for him as a counter-force against Kapwepwe. Both the British and American Governments had seen the political escalation in Northern Rhodesia, from the moment Kapwepwe led his team out of Congress to form ZANC and then UNIP. [...] Kaunda's interview with John F. Kennedy in April 1961 was not fortuitous; it came from [Harold] Macmillan [...]. In this regard, Arthur Wina, who was the [UNIP] representative over there, had done a good job. One thing was clear to him, that in the event of Kapwepwe's long absence from the country in 1960 and 1962, Kaunda would not hold UNIP together — he'd be supplanted by the group which was agitating for Kapwepwe to take over and which Kapwepwe himself kept in check for the sake of achieving unity and independence. It is most likely that Kapwepwe and Kaunda were both aware of this situation. But Kapwepwe was not aware that whilst he welcomed building Kaunda's image, his own [image as a radical] was at the same time being blown out of proportion [...] to Kaunda's satisfaction.

Whether by arrangement or not, Kapwepwe kept aloof from any close friendship with Europeans, even missionaries, leaving that to Kaunda. Although he was a professed agnostic, I noted in his later life that he resented the Scottish Missionaries of his home area and was very partial to Roman Catholics. In playing, as it were, the negative role in the political struggle, in order to produce the dawn of Independence, was Kapwepwe actually anti-white or a Communist? He was neither. What is true is that as far as Europeans in the colony were concerned in politics, he distrusted them all and did not want to appear at anytime to be politically backed by any of them. He felt that they were motivated by financial interest, such that when change came they would support it relative to this. But before then they would hold on to what they had, even if it hurt African aspirations. This attitude proved correct in the 1962 15-15-15 elections, when the European electorate so massively rejected UNIP despite the Party's sustained and sincere campaign to win their support with assurances. [Kapwepwe] had few personal European friends like Simon Zukas, of whom he always spoke highly. His personal views in this respect he did not wish to impose on the party, and he always encouraged Kaunda to explore white support.

Why did humanism begin to turn into political radicalism of a Marxist brand from 1968 onwards? This coincided with Kaunda's [...] differences with Kapwepwe and therefore his attempt to find his own platform. The radicalisation of humanism also coincides with each crisis of his political survival in relation with Kapwepwe or those who looked to the latter for leadership. The Humanism of April 1967 was a response to the already looming struggle for party elections at Mulungushi later that year (August 1967).

When the Humanism ideology did not prevent Kapwepwe's group winning the party elections and the party split threatened his own position, Kaunda announced rather hurriedly the Mulungushi economic reforms, paring to the left. [...] Elections in 1968 did not prove a total victory, and Kapwepwe continued threatening independent authority, so a further step to the left had to be taken, by the 51% takeover of the mining industry; and yet again in 1970 after disbanding the Kapwepwe-dominated Central Committee.

It should be noted how tragically Kapwepwe's long shadow led to UNIP surrendering power to Kaunda. [After the 1967 Mulungushi elections] we have seen fear of Bemba domination, and hence dissolution in 1970 of the Central Committee and substitution of another nominated by Kaunda. Thereafter there has never been an election of the Members of the Central Committee, but an acclamation of a list submitted by Kaunda to the General Council or the National Council. [...] Because any open and free election is still likely to produce the same result as 1967.

The situation from 1972 to date has been a [...] repetition of the history of Zambia, with Kaunda using the same tactics and utterances against Kapwepwe's shadow opposition as Welensky and Arthur Benson did against the nationalist movements.

Appendix 4
Reflections on Governance in the First Republic

From 'The Working of the Civil Service in a Parliamentary Democratic Cabinet'

We inherited a British Parliamentary system together with its Civil Service System with only minimal modifications in political organization. [...] The Governor was a professional Civil Servant and within himself represented the crown or the sovereign in such matters as were delegated by the various laws. He was assisted by the Chief Secretary who functionally headed the Government and the Civil Service. The important thing to note here is that the political and executive arms were fused but the executive was paramount in that it was completely non-partisan and administrative merit alone ensured career development for the colonial officers. This was as it ought to be: the colonies were the direct possession of the crown which had no political party. [...]

Thus the President inherited three roles; those of the sovereign, Head of State and of Government. Without [a] Prime Minister, the Secretary to the Cabinet became effective head of the administration and in general practice of Government, in as much as the President had a fourth and more complicated role — that of head of the ruling party.

The Civil Service is that body of regular (permanent) employees of the State through which the Government executes its functions and obligations to the public and the State itself. [...] It is called permanent [...] in that it provides a means for continuous presence of statehood in a country.

The first Zambian Cabinet was generally able and keen. The Cabinet Secretary attended but could not speak unless asked by the Chairman [President Kaunda]. [...] Cabinet Meetings had priority over all other Government business and I made sure the Chairman never wriggled out of it. [...] They were an interesting affair and members worked with extraordinary jollity together. Only a few did not read their papers and relied on the discussions for them to follow the stream. Some were enthusiastic and read papers thoroughly but the substance was generally above their heads. At a meeting discussing the purchase of a presidential aircraft, just when the recommended model was almost agreed upon, an otherwise capable Minister raised the question of His Excellency's safety — whether or not there should be some defences on board [...], "Can't there be some [bombs or grenades] to throw through the window when necessary?".

There was something of 'scratch my back and I will scratch yours'. Ministers would not oppose a paper by their best friend and vice versa. Some had unfailing loyalty in supporting the opinion of the Chairman.[...] Despite all that rarely was a truly disastrous decision taken; if they went near they corrected themselves later in matters arising.

When I became Secretary to the Cabinet my handicap was not only that I was young but also that I was unknown to most Cabinet Ministers as well as the senior Civil Servants. [...] I had not been to Munali or Chikuni, the two schools to which almost all the Cabinet Ministers and PSs had been; and I had worked in Lusaka for only 6 months before. [...] Few knew my educational and other background and of course they daren't ask. Yet the fact that nobody could remember me at Munali was a sure sign that I had not attained high school and being a graduate was out of the question. The latter was an extremely valuable and important thing to be in those days when there were only a hundred or so. It used to amuse me when in my presence, as if to test me, some Ministers would start enumerating by name the graduates the country had but omitting me.

The Cabinet did not have a single representative from the Copperbelt; those who had been there went as adults seeking employment. Otherwise their backgrounds were the villages and mission schools, plus Munali. To my bitter but quiet annoyance, most of them talked of the Copperbelt like a foreign land full of trouble makers, notwithstanding the fact that it is the copper miner who by and large made independence possible and certainly paid for the regalia of office which they were enjoying. One thing was clear though: they feared the people of the Copperbelt as much as the colonial Government feared them and denied them education to postpone their awakening. It was a sad contemplation that, after all the suffering and the sweat the copper miner had gone through for the country, he could not share in the new political power gained over his head. I was the only son of a miner in a senior government position, most of my friends ha[d] ended education at Standard 4 (the highest class available for a long time on the Copperbelt) and were then lashing copper ore underground to make money to develop the 'Nation'. The same obtained amongst PSs; none had seen the rigours of the suffering of the copper miner who made the reputed wealth of Zambia possible. When they talked of the colour bar and discrimination they made my blood boil because they could only have known its real misery if they had been miners even for a day. I smarted under this resentment throughout my term of office [...].

Appendix 5
Managing Zambia's Finances

From 'The Working of the Civil Service in a Parliamentary Democratic Cabinet'

At Independence or soon after, we naturally lost almost all of the Finance personnel [...]. Regardless of the fact that they were amateurs [in terms of financial expertise], they knew the routines and their sudden departure left a gap that has had a most unfavourable impact on finance administration in Zambia since Independence. In the rural areas, accounts clerks more or less became the finance officers. Even those who had been 'good' in their accounting role were as finance officers handicapped by lack of depth (an educational handicap) and authority (since they were junior in rank). At the HQ, a new but transitory breed of [foreign] economists, most of them young and liberal, took over planning and budgeting, but they either knew nothing about or just ignored financial control. There was not one who previously had experience in public finance, except as theory. Even after they left Zambia not one, to my knowledge, obtained employment with another Government in a similar or higher capacity. Most of them ended up back at the University in the UK completing a PhD thesis based on their experience in Zambia.

Notwithstanding other failings, this group of financial experts had enough educational breadth to have done a good job if, in the absence of grassroots knowledge of the country, they had had the humility to consult those who had, but whom the[y] [...] branded 'colonial conservatives'. Furthermore, their free access to politicians gave them undreamed of power and, I suppose, they must have felt they were fulfilling the role of the mandarins in Whitehall — but without continuing responsibility. As economists they were Keynesian disciples, and the existence of large foreign reserves (£500m) and their rejection of non-deficit budgeting, meant that their advice was to get into deficit and benefit from external aid. Expansion was indeed necessary and inevitable, and some of the investments of the portfolio ridiculous, e.g. into the bonds of City and County Councils in the UK for 99 years at a yield of 4½% etc. The calculation that was absent, however, was the impact of a sudden release of funds into an economy severely lacking in manpower and skills, and the [consequent] impact on Forex earnings. Contractors soon doubled their prices and made sure that each one had enough work. The many new secondary schools increased the already desperate shortage of teachers, and the politicians became aware that even when you are short of money you can budget to spend more without sweat. (There was no incentive to be efficient in spending).

Due to these situations occurring in the first two years of our independence the accounting system to all purposes and intents broke down in 1966. The Ministry of Finance was behind in all accounting returns and checks. Accounts printed out by the computer several months in arrears were wrong. In the latter respect it must be said in fairness that sabotage was not ruled out, as the computer company's HQ was in Salisbury, and the maintenance engineers took their time to come since UDI. And when they came the machine was out [of order] before they reached Salisbury [again]. To correct the situation the PS MF [Ministry of Finance] proposed [to] go to India to hire accountants. [...] The PS concerned [...] by-passed me and convened a meeting with the President, and got the go-ahead. [...] The first batch came out in 1967; by 1969 they had made no impact on the system. Too weak and afraid to resist wrongful instructions from controlling Zambian officers, they stuck to accounts and did not take part in the development planning process. Thus financial management for development remained untackled to date. Unfortunately, the accountants were posted only to Lusaka, and the rural areas had to struggle as best they could, which led to the over-centralisation of the finance function.

By 1980 deficit budgeting, aided by inflation, had run completely out of hand and supplementary expenditure constituted 50% of the budget, because of inadequate control. A combination of poor estimates, lax controls and over-centralisation led to a situation where government cheques or purchase orders were no longer acceptable on sight because they bounced or could not be honoured. The economists in 1965/66 had overlooked (and still do) the fact that Keynesianism had served industrialised nations well only because theirs were the reserve currencies. Deficit budgeting there did not immediately result in shortage of foreign currency and therefore shortages of imported goods [...]. In the seventies Keynesian economics could not cope with the economies of industrialised countries because the OPEC reserves disturbed reserve currency balance, and deficit budgeting began to build up growing unemployment and inflation. For Zambia, such a situation was reached as soon as we wiped out the minimum foreign reserve base in 1974 with the redemption of ZIMCO bonds, and still continued with deficit budgeting, more on the current account than on capital.[1] In addition, most of the foreign aid the country resorted to only went to increase foreign exchange demands indirectly.

---

[1] See also Appendix 13, where this matter is addressed in greater detail.

Appendix 6
UNIP's Mulungushi Elections, 1967

From '1967 Mulungushi Elections'

The 1967 Mulungushi Elections were the first and the biggest threat so far to Kaunda's leadership. His handling of it resulted in 1) tampering with the economy for political rather than economic reasons [...] 2) creating his own political base upon tribal factional fears that resulted in a weak national political administration; naturally secure for himself but unstable for development.

Before the Mulungushi elections he did his best to back [Reuben] Kamanga to retain his Vice-Presidency [...]. Openly he could not back Kamanga, because he would be seen to be anti-Kapwepwe, the 'King Maker'. Kamanga was also being accused of misconduct by his colleagues, which Kaunda was accused of covering up. Kaunda therefore played publicly neutrality as to who was to be elected Vice President [...].

Even by the end of 1966 the pact between Kaunda and the Bembas in the Cabinet was shaky. He was being accused by them of favouring other tribes who did not put him in power. They also blamed him for weakness and drift. In fact, at one Cabinet meeting, [Justin] Chimba mounted what appeared to be a rehearsed attack, ending with a statement that the Government was drifting because it lacked an ideology to direct it. He meant that Kaunda had to decide whether Zambia was going socialist or not. Kaunda took this challenge very seriously, and also as an opportunity to give Chimba a proposition he could not refuse. He called a National Council meeting in Lusaka on 26th April 1967 and announced that the "Zambian ideology is Humanism." Soon after, he transferred Chimba from the Ministry of Commerce & Industry to the new Ministry of National Guidance, for him to direct the nation along the 'Philosophy' of Humanism. He gave him a Minister of State, U.G. Mwila, another Bemba disgruntled and 'overdue' for promotion [...]. Chimba became highly disenchanted and looked to Kapwepwe more and more to take over leadership.

For these elections the Kapwepwe Bemba group deserted their Ngoni allies and joined up with the Tongas. The Ngoni tried to gather up the 'minority' tribes and were working to break up the Bemba solidarity by hiving off the Luapula Bembas, and other Bemba-speakers of Central and Copperbelt provinces. The election of 1967 proved Kapwepwe's dominance. He won, but immediately the results were disputed at Mulungushi itself. When the information was brought to me, I made a quick calculation which confirmed the results, but proposed to Kaunda that the box be sealed immediately and be carted to Lusaka to be recounted by the Chief Justice. The Chief Justice's recount confirmed the results.

This result meant the official Bemba dominance of UNIP and, above all [threatened] Kaunda's security of leadership. The threat, however, brought him allies — the other tribal factions, notably the Lozis, and also the big financial interests which feared Kapwepwe's reputed socialist leanings. Even with the confirmation of the results, the dispute was encouraged to continue, leading Kaunda to abolish the Central Committee and create an interim one.

At a National Council meeting held at Chilenje on Feb 5 1968, the tribal feuding really came to the boil, in an orchestrated anti-Bemba fashion. Having craftily set it up, Kaunda sought a proof of strength or loyalty as far as Kapwepwe was concerned. He stood up and announced he was resigning because he could not be party to leadership divided over tribal lines. He left the hall and went home, after consulting [Chief Justice James] Skinner how he could resign. He was informed of the procedure but did not send his resignation letter. After deliberating the incident, the Council sent Kapwepwe to plead with him to rescind his decision amidst tears from them. Kaunda went back to the meeting.

Tribal nationalism had surely set in, not in the Nation but in the Party leadership who were all fighting to maintain their positions. For Kaunda that feeling was first and foremost an advantage, because he became more of a compromise candidate [...].

Appendix 7
Zambian Humanism

From 'Zambian Humanism'[1]
It was indeed a decade of budding African political thought although, seriously, not one could be called a philosophy. There is no denying that the independence generation of leaders in Africa aspired [...] to establish themselves philosopher kings or at least as men of thoughtful persuasion. After independence the major topic for rallies [i.e. anti-colonialism] was removed. A new rallying point was necessary and the personality of the leader himself was the obvious choice. In this process, it would appear, the leaders confused the monopoly of power with the monopoly of wisdom, and set about to create quotable dicta. Unfortunately the minimal learning most of them possessed deprived their thought of depth, so much so that they had to struggle through a Christ syndrome, because the Bible had been, for the most part, their graduation literature. [...] This aggressive ignorance in small and large measures has stalked Zambia in the last two decades. It was in the background described above that Zambia Humanism as a governing philosophy has its grounding.

At first I was convinced that Kaunda was not serious [in adopting Humanism] and accepted it as his way of shutting up his critics. But he did not only believe in it, but it was being forced on others like gospel: study it for Civil Service exams, a required belief for a citizen to exercise his political and constitutional rights, a portfolio for a whole Ministry, an endowment for a chair at UNZA. [...] In the name of humanism, more money has been spent than that spent by all Christian Churches in Zambia since Independence. It became an article of faith whose only understanding was belief. Under pressure to explain, Humanism has become socialism/communism.

The most fundamental misdirection of premise is the very prefix 'Zambian', denoting Zambians as a unique human species which lived through a special epoch in human history and discovered man and behaved towards him [...] in a manner people referred to as the Westerners never did or do not practice.

---

[1] Here, Musakanya compares 'Zambian Humanism' with the 'philosophies' that various African leaders adopted in the years after Independence, e.g. Ujamaa.

Appendix 8
Kaunda and Colin Morris

From 'Influences on Kaunda'[1]

In 1959, Colin Morris and Mervyn Temple produced the booklet *Black Government?*[2] [...] aimed at correcting Europeans' image of Kaunda, and at the same time starting an image construction campaign which Morris has since maintained in the continued propagation of Humanism as Zambia's national ideology [...]. His efforts have been adequately supplemented by the Rev. McPherson's eulogical biography, *Kaunda of Zambia*.[3] I say eulogical because of its significant exclusion of any critical aspects of his subject and the absence of any complimentary references to Kaunda's associates as leaders [...] e.g. Harry Nkumbula or Simon Kapwepwe.

Black Government?'s [...] main objective was to allay the fears of the Whites, not really about a black Government, but about Kaunda, whom some called 'a black mamba' and whom most just could not trust. Temple and Morris [...] put him forward [...] as a God-fearing Christian. [...] It has since been an almost full-time preoccupation of the Rev. Morris to maintain this image of Kaunda to the world, and [an image of] Zambia as untarnished and abiding of faith.

Kaunda was quoted in *Black Government?* thus: "The demands and aspirations of the majority frighten the minority groups in power, and they react by employing various methods in order to safeguard their privileged positions. They will employ all sorts of methods to keep that power in their hands. As a result police states are created, men lose sight of the most important values and are guided by fear, suspicion and hatred." Kaunda could not have been more right for [this was] the situation he created since 1971, leading to the imposition of a One-Party State in order to keep a UNIP clique and himself in power.

Black Government? set the tone for a relationship which has come to be termed literary collaboration. In fact it is a relationship between a

[1] Here, Musakanya analyses the relationship between Kenneth Kaunda and Colin Morris, and the various published results of their collaboration.
[2] M. Temple (ed.), *Black Government?: A Discussion between Colin Morris and Kenneth Kaunda*, United Society for Christian Literature (Lusaka, 1960).
[3] F. MacPherson, *Kenneth Kaunda of Zambia: The Times and the Man*, Oxford University Press (Oxford, 1975).

prompter/coach and a willing but wayward actor. [...] When Kaunda answers, Morris not only edits the answers but embellishes them with his own philosophy and logic. *Black Government?* clearly shows the disparity in the thought process between the two men. Morris is learned, logically crisp [...] Kaunda's arguments are emotive assertions which, although acceptable from a politician in a nationalistic movement, are lacking in disciplined reasoning. Morris, with both educational and language advantage, is lucid and clearly predetermined to prove and conclude the Kaunda is a "good man" whose half-expressed ideas must be reshaped by Morris in order to be understood and accepted.

In *A Humanist in Africa*[4] [...] Kaunda [reverses] his belief in multi-party politics. [...] There is an [assertion] of a distinct African thought and logic — distinct from 'Western' thought. This begs the question of the generality of humanity and the commonness of rationality, the very justification of equality of man regardless of accidents of colour. But Morris [...] is prepared to agree that what is politically unacceptable in the UK, for example, can be in Zambia; what both condemned in pre-independence should be perpetrated in post-independence. [...] This is not an attitude of mind peculiar to Morris, but many Europeans who are [...] at post-independence African leaders' palaces and also the European governments. As long as they themselves have a friend in the powerful leader, his actions towards his own people, however grotesque, are glossed over as the 'African' way of life.

Morris goes further [...] he rationalises that bad government and injustice are relative depending on who is governing who. [...] Some call this approach 'double standards' but it is in fact racial condescension on his part. [Morris's] position is similar to that of a Stalinist writer-Commissar. He puts forth the theory for good conduct by his medium or power hero and ardently refuses to relate that theory to behaviour. By implication be believes that Kaunda's self-righteousness is completely identifiable with the welfare of Zambia. [...] Any Zambian who is not in the Kaunda 'line' does not even deserve a mention in Zambia. Where Kaunda has riotously violated his avowed principles and good naturedness, Morris has argued passionately that those violations are the new truths and principles [...].

Regarding *Kaunda on Violence*[5]: to those who watched the [Zimbabwean liberation] struggle at close quarters, Kaunda does not come out as a fully principled supporter of that struggle. Due both to his pathological ambivalence and a burning desire to play the leading role, his interventions at times

[4] K.D. Kaunda, *A Humanist in Africa: Letters to Colin D. Morris from Kenneth D. Kaunda*, Longmans (London, 1966).
[5] K.D. Kaunda, *Kaunda on Violence*, Sphere (London, 1982).

nearly wrecked the struggle of the Zimbabweans and it certainly delayed Smith's capitulation. It is no wonder therefore that Kaunda had, rather hurriedly after Zimbabwe's Independence, to exculpate himself by praising and identifying himself unreservedly with armed struggle as a necessary and ultimate solution in the face of political and human oppression. It goes without saying that as a leader of a country and a political system which has lost track with democratic methods of government, he is throwing stones from a glass house.

Unfortunately this is a prescription for violence against all fascist governments, of which by absolute definition there are many in Africa, and Zambia is one of them at the moment. In South Africa it is fascism against the blacks and democracy for the whites. In many African states it is fascism against the majority blacks by a minority ruling elite. [...] As Kaunda himself points out, "The violence of the top-dog (rulers) is often subtle and invisible. It spans a range which takes in international economic pressures, control of the media, manipulation of the education system and psychological conditioning, as well as the more visible strong-arm methods." These are weapons well developed and practiced by Kaunda himself.

Appendix 9
Civil Service, Dispersal and Politicisation

From 'Civil Service, Dispersal and Politicisation'

As early as 1966 the Civil Service was an institution being attacked by the politicians and the visiting paternalistic advisers, ostensibly as being ill-equipped for development administration in the independent state. Whilst the politician spoke ardently of Zambianization, in many cases he intended to mean that this should see an increasing number of his 'home boys' in senior government positions. This was proved by the fact that[...] in 1968 [when] the Zambianization complaints were at their loudest, we had already achieved almost 75% Zambianization. But when more Zambians occupied senior Civil Service positions, the politicians looked upon them as a threat to their power. This was more so given the lack of government experience of most Ministers and politicians.

[...] the expatriates often took advantage of this sense of insecurity. In July 1966, Dominic Mulaisho and Patrick Chisanga, Permanent Secretary and Under Secretary respectively in the Office of the President, were summarily removed from their positions, together with fourteen expatriate Special Branch officers who worked under them. This was on the recommendation of one John Brumer, a Rhodesian double agent, who had infiltrated the President's confidence. Brumer's mission was to disrupt the existing intelligence organization at the time when Rhodesia was setting up its network in Zambia. Mulaisho and I realized early that he was not a person to be relied upon and therefore decided to ignore his advice (which came through the President) concerning organization of internal intelligence. He [Brumer] soon suspected our intuition and told the President that [the] men in charge of intelligence were blocking his advice because they were in collusion with white expatriates who were Rhodesian agents, whom they were retaining in Zambian service. He gave the President the expatriates' names.[1]

In a midnight decision on 14 July 1966, my friends and the 14 expatriates were fired. Amongst the white officers there may have been some with

[1] A more detailed account of the Brumer affair can be found in R. Christie, *For the President's Eyes Only: The Story of John Brumer, Agent Extraordinary* Hugh Keartland Publishers (Johannesburg, 1971).

Rhodesian sympathies [...] but most of them were loyal and they had the advantage of having knowledge of the Rhodesian organization and personnel. [...] Removing them in the manner he did also had an adverse psychological effect amongst the remaining white expatriate Civil Servants, who became gripped by insecurity. [...] It was a successful piece of sabotage which was one of several examples of Kaunda's partiality for private advice from Europeans. In UNIP circles, the July 1966 action served to demonstrate that the permanent senior Civil Servants were not after all that permanent. Although the Zambians were later posted to other ministries in the same capacity, the expatriates' employment was terminated with immediate effect. This was the first time the President dismissed or transferred a Civil Servant.

Early in 1965 it was felt that with the new organization of administration, at Provincial and District level, the party was still not in control, particularly on the Copperbelt. In addition, Kaunda was under some pressure to find employment for a number of Party stalwarts, since they could not all be MPs, Ministers, Ministers of State or Diplomats. The Civil Service demanded some qualifications. So Kaunda thought of [Provincial] Public Relations Assistant [PPRAs] for Ministers of State; I said we could not find room for such a post [...] there was no money. [...] More pressure was put on and finally we made some 'temporary' arrangement for one only, [Fines] Bulawayo for the Western (now Copperbelt) Province. A few days later I was told "he must be provided with Government car" to move around. [...] By 1967, the number of PPRAs (now called Political Assistants [PAs]) had grown to 15. [...] Unofficially, the PA and the Regional Secretary insisted that it was their duty to supervise [...] all Civil Servants [in their provinces and regions]. When the latter resisted such assumptions and pleaded political neutrality as Civil Servants, they were branded as being anti-party. As ANC opposition grew so did UNIP interference in the administration. Kaunda did little about it, but I only realized later that he actually abetted it, anxious to get total control of the Republic and integrate it to fuse all the people into the political system as established by UNIP, to the exclusion of the opposition.

There obviously was a gap of perception between the Civil Service and the politicians. The former perceived Independence, dramatic as it was, as a change of Government which would leave the CS to get on with the job and implement changes in the orderly manner, whilst the politicians should get on with their job of politics. For the politicians, particularly at the lower echelons, Independence was more than that; it meant power, personal power. To step into the shoes and all the trappings of the District Commissioner. To be the one to order the citizens, boot out the 'undesirable' elements. This was the source of the conflict between politics and the administration [...]. Trying to draw the traditional [Western] distinction between the Party and the Government and then the Civil Service, the Civil Servants drew little solace from the President and the Ministers who, deep down, did not trust the CS with its superior jargon of laws and rules. [...] The aggregate of educational assets on the side of the CS versus the meagre one of the Politicians aggravated the cleavage.

The Party remained convinced of the enmity of the Civil Service and that it lay between them and total control of the people. But whilst they politicised the Civil Servants they did not want them in the Party — at least not actively — because they would provide dreaded competition for political jobs. It seemed that the UNIP Government had two options left of dealing with the Zambian Civil Service: 1. Compulsory politicisation (to toe the political line), 2. Remove or retire the hardcore of Senior Civil Servants and replace them by post-independence 'new blood'. That is, mostly those with dubious qualifications from the Eastern Bloc.

The 1964 reorganization of administration and the Party/Civil Service conflict which followed it effectively atrophied the nerve centre of the Administration. With the problems which beset the country in 1965–66 remedial measures could not be taken. In addition, many who were considered capable or useful were withdrawn from districts to the centre to help with the new problems, mostly resulting from UDI, or filling the vacancies created by the rapidly departing expatriates. The result was that by 1967, the Districts were manned by Clerical Officers [acting] as District Secretaries. The Ministers of State with their Political Assistants were of no use to the Administration; on the contrary they ensured that it was paralysed to give way to Party 'supremacy'. In the circumstances, the administrative action was concentrated in Lusaka.

As we have seen, in 1965-66 the Administration was essentially for survival and any thoroughgoing reorganization was inadvisable, even impossible. Nevertheless, some groundwork was being done. Organization and method studies were carried out; comparative studies in the organization of civil services were prepared. There was great concern over financial management, an area where almost all expatriates had left. I spent some time in Canada reviewing the Treasury Board System and brought out an expert to make recommendations for future application to our system. NIPA [National Institute for Public Administration] went into full operation for training [...].

By 1967 the Administration had just emerged from the worst of the crisis and we were prepared to implement long-term reorganization for the Independence Administration and development. [...] But this was not to be! In our or, should I say 'my', concentration on tackling the survival problems, the Civil Service was not aware of the extent of inter-Party factionalism and that against the Civil Service itself. In 1967 the malaise came to the surface.

The fact that in the political process of African participation in Government since 1948, the Bemba were the majority of Africans in the Legislative Council, and were the first Ministers, had never been an issue, even during the nationalist agitation of the 1950s. Of the Permanent Secretaries, only the Bembas had not jumped the queue; they had been in line of seniority by promotion and appointment well before independence. The colonial staff list of 1963 clearly showed that. But Bemba dominance became such a convenient scare that, in my position, it was gradually making my work impossible. It became a handy tool for Kaunda to use against his Bemba rivals, and in the scheme I was designated as one of those.

The campaign that the Civil Service was predominantly Bemba was joined by other regions, each for its own reasons, culminating in an open confrontation at the February 1968 Chilenje National Council. There was no complaint that the CS was inefficient because it had many Bembas. In the process, however, the axe fell on Aaron Milner who, as Minister of State for the Civil Service, was considered unable to control the Secretary to the Cabinet [...] in Bemba-ising the CS. Humphrey Mulemba took over, with instructions from his fellow Ministers to check CS appointments against Bemba bias. He applied the anti-bias [policy] rigorously by requiring to see all my recommendations for appointments and for him to check them personally for merit. He did so for some time, only to admit that he had been misled as to the considerations for appointments. "They could not be fairer", he said, and left me well alone.

From June 1967 to the end of 1968 there were many private consultations conducted by the President without my official knowledge, although I picked up some details on my own. For example, one PS visited my office one day and found me reading a book [...] about the French system of administration — especially the Napoleonic reform of the Prefectures. He asked to borrow it. I lent it to him 'in the interests of the service'. A few days later I found the book on the desk of the President at State House. [...] soon afterwards I began to hear rumours of the changes to take place after the elections which would include the creation of the post of Secretary General to the Government, who would be a politician, [...] a Cabinet Minister and Head of the Civil Service. He would replace the Secretary to the Cabinet. This was a travesty of the French system, where the 'Chef du Cabinet' to the President is a political assistant to the President, and handles his party political affairs and direction of policies. [...] I was appalled by this suggestion because I could not see it working in the interests of efficient administration, but I was given little chance to argue successfully to change some provisions. Since the proposed changes involved abolition of a post I occupied, I gave my resignation from the Civil Service to take effect on the formation of the new Government.

I had earlier cautioned against the President's constant reshuffles of Ministers and PSs, and the splitting and recombining of ministries. He was doing this practically every four months. It led to loss of experience, diminishing job interest and above all, great expense. A major reshuffle cost not less than K250,000. [Musakanya counts 18 reshuffles between 1964 and 1971] Unfortunately, Kaunda has never appreciated nor paid any attention to the implications of financial management. [...] I would request during the preparation of the Budget whether he had any intention to reshuffle Government in the near future so we would take account of it in the estimates. He would reply that he had none at all for some time. A few days or weeks after the Budget was ready, he would announce a reshuffle. There were expenses of movements of whole departments and people from office to office, from one end of town to another or from one end of the country to another. [...] For example he would wish to change one Ministry from one designation to another and allocate it a set of functions. I would point out, if need be, the incompatibility of such function or the inherent disruption to smooth functioning. He would insist to go ahead because "I have thought about it a great deal and it will work better." A few months later he would unbundle. I can only think that he had an idea that he would, by trial and error, one day discover a magic formula of Government[...].

[RE the appointment of Provincial Cabinet Ministers and the related consolidation of central Ministries:] In arguments against this arrangement I pointed out that the resulting effect would be ineffectiveness of Government. The Ministers and their PS's would in the major sectors have too large ministries, too cumbersome for effective control. The Provincial Cabinet Minister who was required to attend Cabinet meetings in Lusaka once a month would have no time for political and administrative work in the province. [...] he would remain with eight days to tour his District and attend to some administrative and statutory meetings. He [Kaunda] said it would work. In fact it ended up with Cabinet meetings happening about once every three months, which resulted in the President making many decisions alone. Even with reduced Cabinet meetings, Cabinet Provincial Ministers spent most of their time either in Lusaka or between Lusaka and the Provincial Headquarters. The Party was strengthened at the Provincial and District levels and the CS accordingly diminished. [...] I pointed out that in the interests of administration, the District Governor (DG) should remain a civil servant who, by amending general orders, would be allowed to carry out some political work. [...] But District Governors were to be former Regional Secretaries of UNIP without educational credentials nor appropriate experience. [...] When [Kaunda] eventually made the appointments there were only three District Secretaries out of 53 DGs and these were very quickly removed. The rest were UNIP Regional Secretaries, generally 'illiterate' who were rewarded for their part in the 'freedom fighting' and would therefore not be bothered about improving themselves by training.

The 1969 reorganization was an admission that persuasion had failed to turn the majority of the Civil Servants into partisans in politics. To the UNIP Government, Civil Service 'political neutrality' was not enough. In fact it was tantamount to opposition; the only acceptable 'neutrality' was to be a card-carrying UNIP member and to deny public services to known members of the opposition. The most compelling reason for the creation of DGs was to enforce such conduct where necessary. It was also thought that should the opposition ANC miraculously win the elections they might find it impossible to get rid of so many DGs [...] and would therefore have a fifth column in their administration. [...] a new Government would have to start all over again to rebuild local administration. The reorganization, as it turned out, achieved complete political control over the country and opposition or resentment against the Party lingered. Kaunda had in 1970 to buy out ANC and ban new parties such as UP [the United Party]and UPP (1971) and expand Special Branch.

Kaunda congratulated himself for this reorganization which, he presumed, politicised the grassroots administration and broke the struggle of the Civil Service by purging those senior civil servants with service connections with the colonial era. It was felt that the major obstacle to independence and development administration had been removed. Almost all persons in influential positions, both in Government and in commerce and industry (Parastatals) were answerable to him; at least they were removable by him at any time. Then, as is the case today, Kaunda was satisfied with the form and never cared for the substance. He was quite certain that as long as there were

Ministers and DGs throughout the country able to harangue the citizenry to work hard and grow more food, the country would buzz with activity. [...] Perhaps it was only Kaunda who was surprised that as the reorganization [...] accelerated, the economy and administration declined. It was a situation where people who had never worked were put in a work position. By their upbringing, they associated work with pick and shovel or hoe and axe, and being placed in a chair behind a desk meant [...] importance for all to behold. That was the reward for organizing UNIP meetings without pay. [...] they were chauffeur-driven around the Boma to show off their GRZ vehicle; collect merchandise 'on credit' from the obsequious Indian shopkeeper; or check on the truant Civil Servant. In the meantime, the services were neglected and Government property deteriorated.

To ensure that Lusaka heard they existed, the people had to be coerced to [local] public meetings, which information personnel must cover and report to Lusaka. The message of hard work and self-reliance was invariably screamed out and, for effect, an attack made on some local reactionary or capitalist (i.e., a civil servant who refuses to attend such public meetings when he was working, or a local businessman who refused 'credit' terms to the Governor). However, the meetings confirmed the Governor's new prosperity. The Party slogans, 'UNIP is power' and 'It pays to belong to UNIP', the peasants who could not sell or transport their produce ruefully but quickly observed.

The 1969 reorganization can be categorised as the beginning of institutional indiscipline and vandalism. By 1980 the cumulative results were the immense scrapyards of Government vehicles averaging three years old. [...] In almost all Government buildings, toilets were blocked off, made unusable through misuse and neglect. The best schools became no better than well-kept pigsties. Although by 1980, expenditure had risen by over 500% over 1970, the Government claimed lack of funds for maintenance. The reasons, however, was there for anybody to observe — the masters were able to spend the money but lacked the minds to create it. The system had not only demoralised the Civil Service; it had removed it from responsibility, which the politician was neither able nor willing to accept.

Appendix 10
The Mulungushi Declaration of 1968

From 'Economic Reforms' and 'Economic Reforms – Continuation'

Although I was convinced [...] that political reasons for personal survival were paramount at the time of each of the economic reforms, a number of genuine reasons for their implementation did exist; but it was politics which dictated the timing and method. Once the political aims appeared satisfied, economics and success thereof bore no consequences.

One of the most deep-seated of racial prejudices is, I think, economic. I do not think I have yet met a white man who has confidence in a black man handling his major economic interests. Thus Europeans cannot have confidence in an African government, however well-meaning. As I have pointed out, at Independence, economics was a closed book to an African. Admittedly there were a handful of wealthy African businessmen, particularly in Northern and Luapula Provinces, but they were only storekeepers or provincial transporters. [...] Otherwise, business and industry was in the hands of European and Asian settlers. [...] Whilst a lot left or sold up soon after Independence, those who remained were determined to benefit from the post-Independence boom, make a quick profit, repatriate it and leave as soon as possible. Our exchange control was virtually non-existent. Profiteering, illegal money transfers and acts of economic sabotage became rampant, and such a threat to our economy that I set up in my office an Economic Intelligence Unit in February 1967. This is today called SITET [Special Investigation Team on Economy and Trade] and is notorious for punitive activities damaging to business and, unwittingly, to the national economy. Despite the Zambian Government's liberal attitude to expatriate businesses, they remained a closed shop and contemptuous of the 'nigger' government. They were known to have adopted a slogan towards African workers—'*Zambia ena Kawena, mali ena Katina*', meaning 'Zambia is yours but the money is ours'.

It was accordingly imperative for Zambia to do something about business. The question was how and when. Towards this solution, I visited Italy during 1966 and 1967 observing the workings of IRI. [...] I concluded, however, that any measure of success depended on government intervention in state enterprise; that nationalisation would be very costly; and finally that we had no manpower. [...] Kaunda appreciated the situation and showed no impatience when he discussed the issue with Sardanis.

The UNIP internal factionalism, which had been brewing since 1966 and which led Kaunda to the declaration of 'Zambian Humanism' in April 1967, did not abate. The August 1967 Party elections which elected Kapwepwe as Vice-President proved this, and increased Kaunda's insecurity. It was soon after this that he instructed Sardanis to work out nationalisation measures, at least in theory. Sardanis was supposed to do this in strict confidence, even excluding me. Kaunda's reasons were that he must be seen to have done the thinking himself; he was already suspicious of me being Bemba; Sardanis and Kapwepwe did not like each other; and Sardanis was not an indigenous Zambian and was white. [Kaunda,] in matters of personal political survival and confidences, trusts only foreigners, especially whites, and Zambians of non-indigenous descent such as himself. It is this tendency which led to his harbouring of the double agent John Brumer, the abject reliance on such people as the late Archie Levin, and of course Colin Morris. The Zambians who have lasted longest in his counsel have had traces of foreign origins. This also applies to the staffing of security services.

Despite the injunction of secrecy, Sardanis discussed bits and pieces of his assignment with me. In principle I agreed that the measure should go ahead, since it would be better handled by him than anybody else, and that further delay could lead to a Tanzanian situation. I however warned that he should be aware that his rationalisation of the matter bore no relationship to Kaunda's motives, which were purely political. If ultimately the political motives did not coincide with economic well-being, he [Kaunda] would not care less provided political aims were satisfied.

I differed from Sardanis on the removal of non-Zambian (mostly Asian) traders from rural areas and second-class trading areas in towns. [...] I argued that, as elsewhere, we were short of manpower, even for individual private enterprise. The type of Zambians likely to make a success of shopkeeping as the Indians did should preferably have at least Junior Secondary School education, but such persons preferred paid employment in Government or the mines to the hardships of shopkeeping, particularly in rural areas[...]. Sardanis' argument was that Zambians had not entered trading because in most areas they faced unfair competition from Asian traders, in addition to their lack of access to capital. He pointed to the success of Zambian traders in the Northern and Luapula Provinces where there were no Asian traders.

Apart from these general discussions, I was not aware of the detail of the plan until its announcement on 19 April 1968 at Mulungushi. This followed the controversial National Council meeting of February 5 1968 at which Kaunda temporarily resigned because of bitter tribal factions. When I received a copy of the measures a day before they were announced, I was appalled by its factual and grammatical errors and stunned by the pervasiveness of the measures. It was obvious that, apart from the economic section written by Sardanis, the introductory sections were pieced together from ministerial submissions and the increasing number of European advisers at State House. Because of the far-reaching effect the measures would have on the economy [...] I had to take fast PR action. With F.H. [Francis] Kaunda I edited the text [...]. It was printed in record time and despatched to Europe and America. When it was announced at Mulungushi, copies were available in European capitals, London and Washington.

Since Government could not be involved in the entire economy, it was an unpleasant necessity for Kaunda to create opportunities for Zambians in the economy. Nevertheless the announcement was laced with warnings to Zambian entrepreneurs-to-be to avoid becoming capitalists and that, should they grow to a certain size, the Government would participate in their business.

A year after the Mulungushi declaration, many shops were closed in the rural areas and the second-class trading areas. There were no Zambians immediately ready to take over the shops. The Asian owners were busy making rearrangements about their businesses — transferring them into the names of relatives or sons with citizenship. Europeans either sold or packed up. This opportunity brought in its wake corruption for the first time in the body politic: corrupt granting of citizenship to Asians; blackmail of Asians to 'sell' businesses to relatives of politicians; political intervention for certain party supporters, either to be granted loans or to have shops surrendered to them. Such instant Zambian businessmen [...] soon shut down, due either to incompetence or a shortage of merchandise which followed the economic decline three years later.

However, in the early seventies, the Zambians (most from Northern and Luapula Provinces) who were 'purged' from the Civil Service or who left Indeco took advantage of the climate created by the Declaration to enter industry and commerce, and became successful. Their success brought new political fears as they created a basis for independent power for people otherwise regarded as hostile to UNIP. New methods were to be used against this group, to the detriment of an economy already past ailing stage. In 1973, one Central Committee member was reported to warn at a meeting that unless "the rising Zambian business class was curbed, it was going to use its money to oust us from power." It was when the Leadership Code was being discussed, with a view to including every Zambian in its provisions. This attitude to native prosperity has always reminded me of a remark made by Nyerere to [Milton] Obote and Kaunda in Dar es Salaam in 1965, in a light-hearted chat at State House. He said, "My boy Kenneth, leave business to foreigners, it is difficult to govern Africans when [they are] prosperous."

The ruling that contracts below K100,000 be awarded to Zambian contractors only led to the closure of many expatriate jobbers, and the rise of Zambians. Two years later, the Government was the victim of its own rule. Many buildings and other works scattered all over the country remained unfinished. The contractors had either run short of money or run away with it. A shortage of materials from 1970 onwards did not help matters. The real problem, however, was that whilst many Zambian contractors were able and experienced artisans, few had any contract management experience. Like the Asian traders, the European small contractors were slowly but surely back in business.

It was the 51% takeovers which were an economic sensation at home and abroad [...]. For UNIP it showed new strength [...] for Kaunda [...] he could tell Europeans to give up their businesses and do so without question! Above all, it meant more jobs to control. The latter subsequently became the basis of Indeco management; Indeco became another branch of Kaunda's interminable reshuffles.

Whatever price was paid for the fixed assets [...] was eventually too high. Most of them had not been replaced [...] since the rumblings of national independence started. [...] Indeco had later to invest a lot of money to overhaul the plant. This, among other things, made Indeco's profitability a serious problem in later years. The country therefore had to spend its foreign exchange [...] three times! Paying for the 51% + management fees, earlier profit repatriations and, later, plant renewal.

Appendix 11
The Mining Takeovers, 1969–73

From 'Matero Declaration'

On 11th August 1969, Kaunda declared the 51% takeover of the Mining Companies despite his disavowal to do so on 19th April 1968, when the first nationalisation took place. [...] he had said at the time to me that he would not touch the mines in the same manner as he had done with the other industries. [...] What made him change his mind? [...] Contrary to expectations, the warnings contained in the Mulungushi reforms and their exemption from takeover [led the] mines [...] to feel that their stay of execution would be short-lived and to draw in their claws as far as development was concerned. [...] The Mines were now rearranging their personnel for dispersal whilst at the same time they redoubled their lobbying for tax restructuring and remittance of dividends. With Sardanis as PS of Ministry of Commerce, Industry and Foreign Trade, a bit more research was done [...] but Chimba, the Minister, was not inclined to listening. [...] To Chimba, anything the Mines sought desperately could only be in their best interest and not that of Zambia.

What brought about the Matero Declaration was politics. The 1968 election results left Kaunda with only two provinces to count on for support: Eastern and North Western. Western (Barotse) and Southern went to the ANC; Northern, Luapula, Copperbelt and half of Central were UNIP [...] not for Kaunda personally, but for Kapwepwe and his followers.

Kaunda's reaction to political crisis is not solutions, but some sort of radical action which may create other problems, but probably less threatening to his own security. So he had one option to mollify the mineworkers, to show them that he was the one in control and not Kapwepwe or Chimba. He removed Chimba from the Ministry and took it up himself, partly because [...] he wanted to make the announcement. [...] the credit was too important to be shared with one whom he knew was opposing him at every turn. [...] He had to show how the philosophy of Humanism had succeeded through the undoubted success of the Indeco operations; that, with 'Decentralisation' introduced after the 1968 elections, which took Cabinet Ministers to rural areas the party was indeed in control of the whole country, so that anybody who had any doubts should forget them.

The intention of the drafters of the 1969 declaration was obviously to tie the loose ends that were left hanging in the air regarding the Mining Industry, and evolve a new policy [with] which to [...] induce the Mines to new expansion programmes, since the restriction on dividends introduced in 1968 did not seem to have moved them at all. These measures were quite certainly not unexpected by the Mining Companies, which took them calmly, whilst intending to play tough in the negotiations, for both the value and the management agreements. The address was warmly received by the Matero audience and also by the African Miners, who earlier in the year had been infuriated by the tough [income] tax measures which Kapwepwe barely cooled with his oratory. Thus, Kaunda came out with laurels by this measure, and his rivals were hard pressed to find ground for discontent amongst the masses [...].

But Kaunda's public gain with the miners was soon ruined, not by his enemies but his ministerial supporters, who in their enthusiasm toured the Copperbelt telling miners and others that "now the Mines belong to UNIP and anyone who does not support UNIP should go." But in the speech Kaunda had spoken and stressed at length the responsible role of MUZ in the new set-up. It was theirs, and they should stop strikes and demands for more pay. [...] feeling stronger, Kaunda occupied himself with resolving the tribal balancing of his Cabinet by demoting or dropping the Bembas to please the factions that were dissatisfied with the 1967 Mulungushi Party elections — he made four reshuffles in 1969.

The Agreements meant a severe forward commitment of Zambian forex, loss of revenue to Government, and a deterioration in due course of the balance of payments [...]. The reorganization of 1973 and the sudden redemption of bonds in that year [...] worsened the situation. In justification, the Government could claim that they paid relatively cheaply for well-developed existing assets. But Justin Zulu, the Governor of the Bank of Zambia, had grave misgivings about the economic wisdom of these transactions.

It is incredible that in a country called a democracy, the President with a few advisors could conclude an arrangement to spend over K240 million of public funds without even a courtesy of laying the terms before Parliament. Not even the Ministry of Finance was legally authorised to supervise the public funds involved. This [elected monarchism] cost Zambia its national sovereignty and plenty of money.

The problems became obvious soon afterwards regarding remittances, because the Mining Companies' accounting was very complex and there was nobody in the Central Bank really competent to unravel them. [...] The Bank of Zambia would be informed by the companies that so much had been paid for copper sold, but it would be put into one of their accounts for several days or weeks, presumably earning interest, before it was transferred to the BoZ account either in the UK or USA.

Mindeco [...] was quite helpless, without enough personnel, both technical and administrative [...] to intervene effectively in the Mine Management. [...] By 1971 we at the Bank of Zambia were worried [by] declining foreign exchange [reserves] caused by the lowest price of copper ever, in the midst of which the Companies wanted their contractual remittances met.

Amongst the arguments against the participation [nationalisation] in the mines under the conditions of the agreement, the strongest was the long-term commitment of foreign exchange against a commodity whose price was independently determined and fickle. [...] As the price of copper plummeted in 1971–92 and [when] Kapwepwe left UNIP (August 1971) to form UPP, these arguments became stronger. Politically the Copperbelt was in 1971–73 lost to UNIP. [...] Kaunda found Kapwepwe's criticism convenient and tacitly shifted the blame for the whole affair onto Sardanis. In the second half of 1972, a team led by Humphrey Mulemba was set up informally to find a way out of the Mines agreements. [...] They must have decided in early 1972 that outright redemption of the bonds was the answer.

The timing of the announcement [of the redemption] was Kaunda's own, and very political in the way of consolidating the One-Party State introduced on 13/12/72 and the constitution signed at the Mulungushi Conference of 25-26 August 1973 [...]. It was the final self-boosting event before the December 1973 elections. Four days later, 31/8/73, he announced the takeover of the management of the Mines and redemption of the Bonds. [...] Those responsible for the takeover of the management were surely not ready [...]. The changeover only took place a year later in 1974. They paid K22m to RST and K33m to Anglo-American in compensation for management. What was the gain? In my opinion they managed to throw good money after bad and dealt a grave blow to Zambia's foreign reserves position.

Appendix 12
Speech to the UNZA Political Association

'The Role of Intellectuals and Activists in Independent Africa',
speech given 10 November 1969

In the African context, rightly or wrongly, it would appear that an intellectual is anyone who has been to school, preferably secondary school, who speaks one of the two official languages, English or French; or better still has been to a University, having scraped through a degree in political science, economics, anthropology, law, etc. (science or engineering smacking too much of manual servitude). Of course, this is crowned with spectacles, golden cufflinks, a golden watch, and similar baubles; knowledge of how to talk to the right person [...] about his country's politics in terms of black and white, of Western and Eastern, of socialism and capitalism, sufficiently self-sufficient to provoke discourse every evening, the intellectual quality being gauged by its verbosity rather than its depth of sense and logic. Also he must be sufficiently sensitive to be hurt by being told the truth, either by his countrymen or a foreigner [...]. The other recent polarisation of intellectual symbolism is the round neck shirt [...] plus a cultivated beard.

Nevertheless, an intellectual activity exists, not perhaps amongst us, but as a human tradition influencing the course of human history. This brand of human being more often than not lives many generations before his time, only to be acknowledged long after his death. [...] An intellectual is universal, both in taste and work; he belongs to human thought generally and not to influences. His works, ideas or aspirations must in their universality endure a period of time and transcend national or racial boundaries. If he fights for freedom in Zambia for Zambians, he will fight in India for Indians, but basically he must fight for human and universal freedom. The endurance of classics, literary and scientific [intellectuals] bears testimony to this. The names of Homer, Socrates, Plato, Virgil, Dante, etc. have come down to us not so much as representatives of their era, but as representatives of the human intellect transcending both time and place.

From this you can perhaps deduce what an intellectual is not. [...] he is not necessarily a conformist, he is not an active revolutionary, he is not indeed a political or social leader, but more of an individualist. [...] as soon as an erstwhile intellectual embraces group philosophy he thereby ceases to play the role of an intellectual [...]. The words 'intellectual' and 'activist' are therefore exclusive — you can only be one or the other.

You will probably have noted that from my description of an intellectual, I have almost eliminated his existence in the African social system so far, because he has failed to ensure his individual existence by originality, universality and creative work. It would appear that the African intellectual [...] seeks his acknowledgement in an active participation in the social order [...]. Consequently he transfers himself into an activist far too early in his intellectual development. [...] If African intellectuals emerge, the only useful role they could play, to my mind, is that of independent, free non-partisan and fearless commentators or scholars; to maintain their intellectual honesty and integrity [...] they must constantly guard against a greedy eye for self-aggrandisement or the rewards of public office. This approach will, without doubt and quickly, earn the intellectual [...] the now normal ostracising epithets of 'sell out', 'colonial/imperialist stooge', 'elitist' [...].

[..]I must give what I consider to be some of the reasons inhibiting intellectual expression and growth in Independent Africa. Firstly as I have indicated earlier, no sooner have the few who have potential attempt[ed] intellectual self-assertion, than they are either corrupted by greed and the pomp of office, or are turned into activists to implement the accepted theories of long-established schools of thought, divided into the various ideologies well-known to the world today. [...] claimants to intellectual leadership in Africa try to acquire their reputation by repetition of well-exhorted theories on African socialism, African personality, Colonialism, Capitalism, culture, etc., and in all cases hardly developing these 'isms' an iota further.

Secondly, and probably the most debilitating handicap [...] is that very early in the formative years the African countries tend to throw up philosopher Presidents who, naturally enough, publicly put forward their social and political views. [...] these views rapidly assume positions of national philosophies with the consequence that any attempt by anybody [...] to subject these views to critical analysis is liable to be interpreted as evidence of gross disloyalty to the State. For example, it was not safe at the height of President Nkrumah's administration for Ghanaian intellectuals to pass comment on President Nkrumah's doctrines of Pan-Africanism or Consciencism. Equally it is not prudent to attempt to subject President Senghor's philosophy of Negritude to a too critical analysis, nor President Nyerere's African Socialism or President Kaunda's Zambian Humanism to a too close scrutiny, unless of course such scrutiny is directed at confirming why such philosophies are not only right but highly desirable. It is dangerous to flex one's intellectual muscles in these fields; not that their authors are likely to react strongly, but the rank and file will almost certainly see to it that you toe the line. Consequently the African intellectuals today tend to be simply apologists of National philosophies.

In this frame of mind [the African intellectual] virtually regrets having been to school at all and he joins in the general condemnation of the educated as the enemies of national aspirations. He packs up objectivity and is led into gestures of national delusions, foregoing any form of constructive criticism. Such intellectual traitors are pathetic, but independent Africa is now riddled with them; their worth is exaggerated out of all proportion by the close ear given them by the deluded do-gooders of this world, which only serves to heighten the conceit of the would-be intellectual.

Appendix 13
Rural and Urban Development

From 'Humanism and Economic Development'[1]

Rural Development:

I have previously gone on record (1969) [regarding] the inevitability of nugatory expenditure of public funds if Rural Development is, for its own sake, a priority, to the relative neglect of urban areas. I added that such a distinct approach to Rural Development should exist only as an integral part of national development. I received rude condemnations for these views which were twisted on political platforms [to suggest] that I was against Rural Development. I feel that my views still stand valid; after twelve years of lavish expenditure [...] rural areas have declined and the towns have increased in population, causing squatter settlements now beyond the Government's ability to control.

A society, to be developed, does not necessarily have to possess all or most of the natural resources within its geopolitical boundaries. What is absolutely necessary is that the people should, through good (as opposed to mere utilitarian) education, be so developed as to use their abilities and initiative to the utmost advantage of themselves and their community.

When the Africa-lovers, led by the indefatigable Prof. [Rene] Dumont, swarm the African Heads of States' palaces, advising the Presidents of the prime importance of developing the rural areas, they are both right and wrong. They are right that it is from the rural areas [...] that the urban areas spring and draw their vitality; they are wrong because their conception of the rural areas stems from their home experiences and they are vastly different to ours.

It is a sociological imperative that human beings tend to gravitate towards larger concentrations of their fellow human beings — thus towns and cities grow and comparatively fewer people remain in the rural areas. The end result of any successful development of a rural area is the growth of an urban area. With all their disadvantages, urban areas are an inevitable consequence

[1] Here, Musakanya offers his critique of Zambia's model of post-Independence economic development, and outlines his own.

of advancement. Conversely, the rural population usually becomes more productive because it is no longer entirely rural, but an agrarian industrial rural population. [...] however large a peasant population it may be, it is rarely able to feed the nation. [...] urbanization cannot be fought successfully; neither can rural-to-urban drift, except by undemocratic regimentation and at the expense of a normal rate of progress.

It is in large population centres that the individual's wits and intellect seem to meet the challenge, as they are pitted against many others in the race of survival of the fittest. It is there that those of talent show up and can be acclaimed; otherwise many a genius has lived and died in the rural communities, a total loss to humanity. This becomes a process of natural selection [...]. Those who make it modestly in rural areas feel an urge to go and try it out in the city [...]. Even the politicians who clamour in many parts of the world for a return to the countryside do so from crowded cities.

We can look at Zambia in light of the above [...]. By the beginning of World War II there started a rural-urban migration to the line of rail, mostly the able bodied young men and women. Most of them went to the Copperbelt, some to Rhodesia and South Africa. By the '60s over 50% of the population had left most provinces with the exception of the Southern and Central provinces. Otherwise only old men, women and children remained in the villages. The village, as idealised in Zambian Humanism, had gone a long way to disintegration. At first, men left their wives behind and worked for a stint of usually six months and rejoined their families at the village. But by the mid-forties, wives were instead joining their husbands in large numbers, and 'Compounds' for married workers soon exceeded those of the unmarried. A lot of those families have made the Copperbelt their home and have their third generation there. Those who retired found their former villages broken up, their age-mates dead and were more than strangers in their own areas. Worse still, they were unable to revert to the village agricultural routine. Accordingly, many 'machona' still remain in the urban areas, swelling the shanty towns whilst villages remain depleted of able-bodied men. The expression of the tradition of assisting the parents and the extended family became the remittance of a postal order once or twice a year. This died away with improvements in transport, which enable the 'old people' to visit their children in town instead.

Since for development you need people, you must obviously start from where the potential of numbers is greatest and expand from there. [...] all the land near the urban areas should be properly surveyed and apportioned for development. Provide [an] intensive communications network, power, health and education services, and above all [agricultural] extension services. In this case the Government would not be overstretched with regard to these services. This idea is by no means new; it was used by the colonial Government for European settlement in agriculture [...]. For Lusaka and Kabwe, Chalimbana and Chisamba areas were created. For the Copperbelt, 'small holdings' were created near each town. As the towns expanded, these peri-urban farms went further and old ones became suburbs: Kabulonga, Misundu, Garneton etc. Those who need larger farms will naturally move further away from the urban areas [...]. In the process suggested, the country can harness agricultural labour which now goes to waste after retirement.

The same approach should be made to provincial capitals in rural areas. Agricultural settlement lands would be serviced and made available near the town. Villages will have to be moved further afield. There will be those who will wish to retire near home and [they] should be given the option and assistance to do so. The colonial government tried this approach in regard to rural areas, but made a cardinal error in trying to create artificial satellite towns as the nucleus for agriculture e.g. Mungwi, Nakashende near Kasama and Mongu, instead of expanding the towns themselves and creating the small-holdings around them [...]. Can you imagine what would have happened now if the infrastructure placed at Mungwi — the schools, clinics etc. — had been added to Kasama and the farms nearby? A larger marketplace could have been created by attracting even more individual expansion [...]. Towns are rarely made, they become.

In my proposals in 1969/70 I [...] referred to the creation of Intensive Development Zones — meaning certain rural areas, with adequate population density and an especially identified population, should receive special planning attention to exploit its potential. I received sneers and concentrated abuse from the Office of National Development Planning (ONDP) which rejected all I had said. But some years later the rural areas were crawling with notices marked 'IDZ'. Up to now I do not know which areas came under the IDZ programme and I have not seen the results; probably the programme ended when the Land Rovers were wrecked.

The Zambian leadership continues to think that their responsibility as to policy begins and ends at vocal 'mobilisation' of the people as to what the Government wants to be done, not how and when it should be done. 'Rural development' has been priority number one since Independence but the results have been declining production and further rural exodus.

In the sting of ministerial reshuffles the Ministry of Agriculture has suffered just as badly as the rest, although one would have thought one way of showing commitment to the agricultural priority would have been ministerial stability and quality; only two ministers of real competence have briefly held that portfolio — Sipalo and Chikwanda. Even the methodology has been a matter of dispute, largely due to the conflicting foreign advisers' opinions — namely whether or not mechanisation is acceptable [...]. Anyone with knowledge of our climatic conditions and has serious agricultural experience knows that there is no alternative to intensive mechanisation for successful and productive farming on a big scale.

'Cooperatives' are another example of terminological misappropriation. Kaunda has often emphasised and is himself convinced that Cooperatives are part of the African way of life [...]. Yet all the evidence is to the contrary; the Cooperative concept itself is Western and it is there that it has had some measure of success [...]. Even in business, companies or corporations have been, amongst Africans, generally individual ventures. [...] accordingly they do not do well and usually die with the individual. The strength of feeling of clan and tribal cohesion (as against nation) in Africans is a secondary symptom of that individualism [...]. But individualism is not negative or unprogressive, except when it is artificially suppressed. Calling a personal subsistence existence a 'Cooperative' [...] cannot be construed to mean a cooperative in the legal sense.

Appendix 14
Letter to Malcolm Christie, February 1970

Letter to Malcolm Christie, February 1970[1]

[...] the best strategy for Zambia is to start agricultural and rural development from the centre of industrialised and economic activity represented by the railway spine and the already 'urbanised' rural administrative centres [...]. We have in Zambia the Great East Road and the Great North Road which cut through large stretches of land uninhabited on either side and land [which] is not in all cases infertile. The roads are in my opinion good enough communications as an incentive [to agricultural activity] and the population could well have taken advantage of them.

[...] you assume that commodity incomes in the rural areas in the developed countries slow down the drift to the urban areas. The facts of rural urban migration in the last ten years do not support this viewpoint. [...] many developed countries have still to pay subsidies to their farmers [...] to keep them on the land and improve production, but, of course, succeeding in neither!

I agree with you that should the present state of rural-urban migration continue, which I am afraid it will, there will be a very large population in the urban areas by 1986. But it does not necessarily follow that half the 'labour force' there will be unemployed unless, of course, we [continue to] regard the Zambian urban dwellers [as] non-citizens of these areas, [...] continue to register them according to their village origins and hoping that they will go back to their village. This they will not do.

I am not against rural development as such, but that approach that defines rural development by the greater distance from the urban areas and unwittingly regarding the urban areas as alien parts of Zambia. This approach ruralisation; mine is urbanisation of the rural areas, and the easiest targets are those unoccupied lands immediately adjacent to the urban areas [...]

---

[1] Musakanya, during his period as Minister of State for Technical and Vocational Education, had written article on his views regarding rural development. Christie, a senior official at the Ministry of Finance, commented critically on the article, defending the existing policy of attempting to close the rural/urban gap etc. In this letter of 6 February 1970, Musakanya sets out and further justifies his argument for a focus on peri-urban development along the line of rail.

If you look at the patterns of land settlement before Independence, the farmers were in those areas immediately adjacent to the urban areas. Whilst they enjoyed the incomes of intensive farming, they were in close proximity to the urban areas and shared its advantages and amenities [...]. The situation here today is that most of these farms have been abandoned and are unproductive [...]. What is required at present is prompt parcelling of those lands into manageable plots, varying in size, and use the plots. There is, of course, at present some timidity towards tackling the land tenure issue, but should the hand be forced at a later date it will be done chaotically.

This approach [...] I have no doubt could be immediately productive and will go a long way towards solving the so-called squatter problem. Its major ingredient would be the husbanding of the scarcest commodity, i.e. the developed manpower which is at present almost 100% in the urban areas [...]. After all, what we want is productivity for self-sufficiency, and later for export, and the nearer therefore the bulk of production takes place to established populations and communications, the better and cheaper [...]. Tribesmen will not easily abandon their areas to settle in the new ones I am proposing, but it is in nobody's interests to encourage tribal holdings, and we have also a duty to provide land occupations for the floating detribalised populations now in or near the urban centres and the line of rail, who in the absolute sense are the majority.